"Patric Knaak's *On Mission* is a wonderful resource not only in helping short-term missionaries prepare, reflect, and debrief their short-term missions experience but to draw closer to our Lord Jesus Christ."

Lloyd Kim, Coordinator, Mission to the World

"Patric Knaak's devotions are wonderful for the spiritual preparation, encouragement, and reflection that should accompany (and follow) mission trips. His thoughtful, vulnerable, and clear explanations of the impact of the gospel on his heart during the 'stretching' experiences of mission work provide intriguing reading and inspiring thoughts for those who want Christ's identity to transform their own hearts, as well as save the souls of others."

Bryan Chapell, Author of *Christ-Centered Preaching*; pastor, Grace Presbyterian Church, Peoria, IL

"Patric Knaak has been on a lifelong journey to further God's mission. With humor, transparency, and wisdom *On Mission* deals with the issues he has faced and lessons that can be learned on the missionary journey. Patric's book will help the reader deal with practical challenges that require God's grace while on God's mission. I commend *On Mission* to all who would follow Christ in leaving the comfortable certainties of the home culture to spend time and effort in what will seem a strange and challenging yet enriching mission experience."

Paul McKaughan, The Ambassador at Large, Mission Exchange

"Short-term mission trips are often surprisingly powerful, life-transforming experiences for those who go. Why? Because God takes pleasure in bringing honor to his Son by displaying his presence and power to those who align their purposes with his for the nations. When followers of Christ leave their comfort zones, even for a brief period on a short-term mission trip, they are often forced to face their fears, arrogance, and foolishness. However, most have not been adequately prepared to embrace their weaknesses in a way that leads them to deeper levels of dependence on Christ and intimacy with him. That's why I'm grateful for Knaak's *On Mission*. It's a comprehensive, gospel-centered resource designed to help you encounter Jesus in unique ways before, during, and after your mission trip. I highly recommend it."

Dr. Steve Childers, Professor of Practical Theology, RTS-Orlando; President and CEO, Pathway Learning

"I highly recommend this new book that provides devotions for short-term missionaries while on their mission. Each Bible study helps them focus on Jesus to strengthen their relations with fellow missionaries and the people they serve. It also includes methods of debriefing after returning home, with studies to assist them to continue in mission while at home."

John E. Kyle, Wycliffe Bible Translators, Philippines and USA; Founding Director, Mission to the World; Missions Director and VP of InterVarsity Christian Fellowship USA; Senior VP of the Evangelical Fellowship of Mission Agencies

"It is generally easier to get people logistically prepared for a mission trip than to help them prepare spiritually. This small book is quite remarkable because it helps prepare you for your short-term trip spiritually and also relationally. And it does this in a very reflective way by providing thoughtful devotional resources for your trip as well as a debrief. Short-term trips provide a great opportunity for service and the spiritual formation of those who go. This book helps make that formation intentional and gospel-driven."

James C. Wilhoit, Scripture Press Professor of Christian Education, Wheaton College

"This is the devotional I wish I'd had for so many short-term trips in the past, and it's the one I hope future short-term teams will carry with them when they come. It's a daily, poignant, and personal reminder that God's mission isn't first 'out there'; it is first to me, 'in my own heart.'"

Cartee Bales, MTW International Director, Asia/Pacific

"Accessible and helpfully formatted, *On Mission* realistically identifies the challenges of mission teams, especially cross-cultural ones. Through looking at a number of stories and incidents from the life of Jesus, it focuses on applying the transforming good news about Jesus to the heart rather than simply offering skills or techniques. It also provides important encouragement for debriefing, including helpful material on how to tell your story. The final sections ensure that readers are encouraged to think about how to develop as world Christians rather than just seeing the trip as a self-contained event. I hope this short book is widely circulated, and I can see its first users/readers becoming the best publicists."

Cassells Morrell, International Fellowship of Evangelical Students Associate Regional Secretary for Europe

ON MISSION

Devotions for Your Short-Term Trip

Patric J. Knaak

New
Growth
Press

WWW.NEWGROWTHPRESS.COM

New Growth Press, Greensboro, NC 27404
Copyright © 2015 by Patric J. Knaak

Cover Design: Faceout Books, faceoutstudio.com
Typesetting: Lisa Parnell, lparnell.com

ISBN: 978-1-942572-12-1 (Print)
ISBN: 978-1-942572-13-8 (eBook)

Printed in the United States of America

22 21 20 19 18 17 16 15   1 2 3 4 5

CONTENTS

After the Trip

ACKNOWLEDGMENTS

Content creation at Serge is always a bit of a team effort and I've been blessed to serve on a team with others who have challenged, inspired, helped, and encouraged me deeply. Lindsay Kimball has freely shared her time, brainstormed topics, offered suggestions, organized my rambling thoughts on occasion, and never failed to provide me with great ideas about how to make things better. Josiah Bancroft and Jeff McMullen have listened to me think through ideas and offered great insight into the exegetical parts of *On Mission*. Karen Herold has steadfastly read every word, organizing, and reformatting the early drafts. Sue Lutz, my editor, has given invaluable help in sharpening and clarifying the content. Barbara Juliani and her team at New Growth Press have been wonderful dialogue partners and have done an exceptional job of guiding me through this project. Without Barbara's encouragement and vision for the project, it never would have happened.

BEFORE YOU GO

INTRODUCTION: LEARNING TO SHOUT

I've always been drawn to scenes from the life of Jesus, where seemingly random people wake up in the morning expecting nothing but their normal lives but end up coming face-to-face with the second person of the Trinity. One of my favorites is Jesus's encounter with Bartimaeus, a blind man forced to beg for his living. You can read it for yourself in Mark 10:46–52.

The assumption of the day was that Bartimaeus (or someone very close to him) had sinned gravely and thus God had punished him with blindness. Begging, especially by someone who is just "getting what he deserves," would have been difficult and demeaning work, offering little more than subsistence living. But in this case it has also done something else: it has prepared Bartimaeus's heart in a unique way to encounter Jesus. That's the intent of this book too—to prepare our hearts to encounter Jesus in unique ways as we embark on the intensity and challenges of a short-term mission trip.

I have to say, though, that in my most tender moments with God, I am rarely as "abandoned" as Bartimaeus is when he encounters Jesus. I'm too embarrassed by my needs and inadequacies to start screaming out my deepest desires to Jesus. Far too often my unbelief muzzles my desperation and I fail to cry out in faith to the One who has poured out his lifeblood for me. Instead, I tend to ask for things politely, from a distance, outlining items that I think I *should* want as a spiritually mature person instead of pouring out my heart when Jesus asks, "Patric, what do you want me to do for you?"

Not so with Bartimaeus. He runs in faith to Jesus with his deepest desires—that by faith he can be made right, reconciled to his God and Father, healed of his blindness and, as a result, released from his life as a beggar. He literally shouts louder than the rest of the crowd as Jesus, God's Forever King who will sit on David's throne, passes by. There is no pretense or artificiality in him. As a man whose blindness has forced him to ask for everything instead

1

of trying to earn it for himself, Bartimaeus is free from the illusion of his own adequacy and control. Instead, he *asks*—boldly and loudly.

Mission trips give us a unique opportunity to see and experience God differently than we do at home. Away from the demands of "normal" life, things come into focus differently. Our need for God's provision is more evident. Jesus's words echo a little more clearly. God's passion to see others redeemed is on display. Short-term mission trips have shaped my walk with Jesus in deep and profound ways. In fact, they are a large part of why I work for a mission agency today.

It's my prayer that your trip will be a truly life-changing event and that you, like Bartimaeus, will experience the freedom that comes from shouting out your deepest needs to the One who is able to meet them.

HOW TO GET THE MOST OUT OF *ON MISSION*

On Mission is designed to be a comprehensive spiritual resource for your short-term mission trip. At the heart of *On Mission* are ten daily devotionals specifically written for individuals and teams participating in short-term mission work. But *On Mission* also contains material to help you prepare for and debrief after your trip, travel features to give you a place to record the details and memories of your adventure, additional ideas for devotionals and journaling, and lots of extra pages to let you capture your experiences and conversations with God.

BEFORE YOU GO

INTRODUCTION
A basic introduction to *On Mission* and an overview of its features.

PRE-TRIP EXERCISE: READY OR NOT?
Designed to help you identify some of your needs and hopes going into the trip. *Ready or Not?* will also give you the chance to journal about things you'd like to see God do on your trip and to craft a prayer update to send out before you leave.

TRAVELOGUE FEATURES: MY TEAMMATES; HOLDING THE ROPES
My Teammates and *Holding the Ropes* provide easy ways to record the names and contact information for your teammates and your supporters.

ON THE TRIP

DAILY DEVOTIONS
On Mission's daily devotionals are designed to help you connect with Christ in deep and refreshing ways as you experience the highs and lows of your

journey. Every day begins with a passage from the Gospels that focuses on Jesus. A brief article provides the content for each day and is followed by thought-provoking questions and prayer and journaling exercises. Each devotional also includes a reflection section where you can record how you saw God work during the course of the day. Because they can be completed in thirty minutes, the devotionals are easy to schedule consistently throughout your trip.

ADDITIONAL DEVOTIONAL RESOURCE: INTRODUCING *LECTIO DIVINA*

For trips lasting longer than ten days, the *Additional Devotional Resource* section will help you use an ancient method of devotional reading that combines Scripture and prayer into an intimate listening experience with God.

TRAVELOGUE FEATURES: OUR JOURNEY; NEW FRIENDS; MISSION MEMORIES; BY THE NUMBERS

Our Journey, New Friends, Mission Memories, and *By the Numbers* all provide handy ways to record the unique memories, people, and experiences you'll encounter along the way.

AFTER THE TRIP

God's work in your life doesn't end when you return home. In many ways, it's just beginning. To help you make the lessons of your trip last a lifetime, the debrief exercises will help you record and organize your thoughts, listen more intently to God, and discern his plans for you as you think about the future. They will also help you continue to live *on mission*—with the same outward focus of helping others meet Jesus that you developed during your trip.

DEBRIEF ONE: MAKING SENSE OF WHAT YOU'VE SEEN

Completed on your journey home or in the first week after you're back, the first debrief will help you to record the spiritual lessons of your trip while they are fresh and to reflect on all the ways that God was at work during your trip. It will also help you prepare to tell your story to your church, friends, and supporters.

DEBRIEF TWO: THE GOSPEL IN AND THROUGH YOU

Completed four to six weeks after you're back and the dust has settled, the second debrief is geared toward helping you connect the experiences and lessons of your trip with your daily life. It features a planning section designed to help you come up with some concrete ways to live more missionally—to pray, serve, give, and go in ways that will help others see Jesus more clearly—as part of your normal lifestyle.

DEBRIEF THREE: THE ONGOING JOURNEY

Completed six months after your trip, the final debrief will help you review your plans and consider additional ways to be missionally engaged, involved in helping God's kingdom grow and new people find Christ.

PRE-TRIP EXERCISE
Ready or Not?

To be done one week pre-trip

As you prepare to leave for your mission trip in the next week, it's likely that you are feeling a wide range of emotions. Often, getting ready to do ministry in a different cultural context can bring out strange paradoxes in our hearts. We can, at the exact same moment, feel excited about what God will do in and through us, and yet slightly panicked at the hundreds of unknowns that lie ahead. If you're feeling this spectrum of emotion this week, you're in good company!

PART 1: INVENTORY OF NEEDS AND HOPES

Take a few minutes in the busyness of packing and checking off your pre-trip "To Do's" to take an inventory of your needs and hopes for your trip. Then answer the questions below.

Afraid

☐ Of the unknown

☐ Of entering an unknown culture or situation

☐ Of being away from family and home

☐ Of having to do things that will be hard

☐ Of being asked to eat "disgusting" food

☐ Of not knowing what I'm doing

☐ Of feeling unprepared or incapable

☐ Of making mistakes, making others angry

☐ Of getting hurt or sick

☐ Of my prayers not being answered

☐ Of my family getting hurt or sick while I'm gone

☐ Of not having enough privacy or down time

Under Pressure

☐ To not let others see my sin and fears

☐ To be perfect (or cover it up if I'm not)

☐ To see lives changed/people get saved

☐ To not let my teammates/family down

☐ To produce big results to report after the trip, especially since many are supporting me

☐ To be a great leader who knows just what to do and how to do it

☐ To be a great teammate who doesn't complain or cause any trouble

Excited

☐ New place, new people

☐ New experiences and culture

☐ This will be my first _____

☐ Seeing God work in special ways in my life

☐ Seeing God change people/bring them to faith

☐ Going with a group and making new friends

☐ Going with my family and bonding together

Hopeful

☐ This will be "the experience of lifetime"

☐ I'll be changed; things will never be the same

☐ God will do amazing things

☐ I won't be as sinful as I normally am

☐ Our team can make a real difference

☐ God will be glorified through me

Expecting

☐ To really help others and be used by God

☐ To see my spiritual life deepen

☐ To experience renewed intimacy with God

☐ To see God work in ways I often overlook

☐ To be part of God's kingdom in a different way

1. As you prepare to leave, what are your biggest fears?

....

....

....

....

....

2. Is there anything about the trip that makes you uneasy in "the pit of your stomach" when you think about it?

....

....

....

....

....

3. In what ways are you feeling needy?

....

....

....

....

....

4. What are your hopes and expectations for this trip?

....

....

....

....

....

5. What are you excited about seeing God do in you and through you?

....

....

....

....

....

PART 2: TALKING WITH GOD

Using the inventory and answers to the questions above, write a letter/prayer to God. Tell him about your needs and fears, your hopes and expectations as you head into this trip. As you write, consider:

- What do you want to see God do in you on this trip?
- Where are you feeling like you will have a hard time trusting God?
- What would you like to see God do through you on this trip?

PART 3: EMAILING YOUR SUPPORT TEAM

Nothing is more critical than to have a group of friends, family, and supporters who will pray for you daily while you are away. Using some of the concerns you've identified and some of the things you'd like to see God do on the trip, write them one short, final email, letting them know how they can pray.

GUIDELINES

1. Be Honest: People will pray for you if they sense you are needy. So let them know what your needs really are, not just the surface issues. Use the work you did in Parts 1 and 2 to guide you about what to include.
2. Be Short: You want people to be able to read your email quickly and pray specifically. A few sentences followed by a list of four to seven things is great.
3. Be Thankful: Every single person on your list is someone special to you, someone who cares about you and who is going pray for you. Let these people know how thankful you are for them.

TRAVELOGUE FEATURES

God has brought together just the right people at just the right time to accomplish the very things he wants to see done on your trip! Take a few minutes before you go, or early on, to record everyone who is on your team. Be sure to include any key on-site leaders where you will be serving (i.e. nationals, missionaries, people who run the long-term ministry on site, etc.).

Over the course of the trip, look for qualities or experiences that make you grateful for each person. During your time together, if you have the patience to look, you'll find out you're serving alongside of some pretty amazing people!

Don't forget to get contact information so that you can easily stay in contact once you return.

MY TEAMMATES

Name	Why I'm Grateful for This Person	Contact Info

Name	Why I'm Grateful for This Person	Contact Info

Name	Why I'm Grateful for This Person	Contact Info

HOLDING THE ROPES

Before British missionary William Carey set out for India to share the gospel in the late 1700s, he famously said, "I will go down if you will hold the rope." Who are those back home who are "holding the rope" for you during your trip? Who are those on your team of prayer and financial supporters? As you list their names here, you'll be amazed both now and in the future at how God faithfully provided a multitude of supporters to come alongside you and send you out. Use this list to follow up with your home team after your trip.

Name	Contact Info

Name	Contact Info

JESUS IS THE ONE WHO SUSTAINS YOU

I distinctly remember preparing for the first mission trip I ever took. I was in high school. A friend and I had signed up to spend an entire summer overseas doing outreach. As a new Christian, I was absolutely certain that this trip would be the secret ingredient that lit my spiritual life on fire. I assumed that my devotional life would blossom and I'd overcome all of those pesky "signature sins" that seemed to characterize my everyday life. No more doubts, no more struggles, no more setbacks. Just the "new and improved Patric," going to tell the rest of the world that they needed Jesus—big time. Imagine my surprise when I discovered that all of the same sins, doubts, and struggles had followed me to the field. In many ways, they seemed worse than ever!

That summer *was* one of the most spiritually formative events in my life, but in none of the ways I thought it would be. The lessons I began to learn that summer have taken many years to mature and bear fruit. But the enduring memory of that summer is that this was when I started to understand that my sin was a lot more deeply ingrained than I had ever imagined and, at the very same time, I was more loved by God than I ever dared to hope, all because of Jesus.

For the next ten days we're going to spend some time looking at scenes from Jesus's life. Each one will present us with the unique ways that Jesus meets and connects with us, particularly as we step out to walk with him on mission.

Date: ....

Location: ....

How I'll Be Serving Today: ....

....

....

BIG IDEA

Most of the time, we think of connecting with Jesus as carving out a few minutes for devotions or prayer. But Jesus sees our connection with him in terms of a living, breathing, growing, moment-by-moment relationship, apart from which we can do nothing.

MEETING WITH GOD *(15 Minutes)*

I AM THE VINE (JOHN 15:1–11[1])

[1] "I am the true vine, and my Father is the gardener. [2] He cuts off every branch in me that bears no fruit, while every branch that does bear fruit he prunes [trims clean] so that it will be even more fruitful. [3] You are already clean because of the word I have spoken to you. [4] Remain in me, as I also remain in you. No branch can bear fruit by itself; it must remain in the vine. Neither can you bear fruit unless you remain in me.

[5] "I am the vine; you are the branches. If you remain in me and I in you, you will bear much fruit; apart from me you can do nothing. [6] If you do not remain in me, you are like a branch that is thrown away and withers; such branches are picked up, thrown into the fire and burned. [7] If you remain in me and my words remain in you, ask whatever you wish, and it will be done for you. [8] This is to my Father's glory, that you bear much fruit, showing yourselves to be my disciples.

---

1. Throughout the devotionals, I have used the NIV translation for the Scripture passages. However, in some places I have included text in brackets that I believe better captures the intent of the original language.

⁹ "As the Father has loved me, so have I loved you. Now remain in my love. ¹⁰ If you keep my commands, you will remain in my love, just as I have kept my Father's commands and remain in his love. ¹¹ I have told you this so that my joy may be in you and that your joy may be complete.

YOU CAN DO NOTHING (AT ALL)

In today's passage, Jesus is talking to his disciples on the evening before his arrest. He will be crucified the following day. He knows that the disciples are getting ready to start doing ministry "on their own," without him physically present to lead, instruct, and guide them, so he wants to be sure that the lessons he has been living out with them for the previous three years are crystal clear. After all, the disciples didn't have a stellar record up to this point.

In speaking about his connection with the disciples, Jesus uses a metaphor that would have been readily understood by all: that of a vine, its branches, and the fruit it produces. Everyone present that night would have been familiar with the thick, gnarly, stout vines that looked a lot like the picture below. When Jesus says that he is the vine, he's referring to the woody, stout trunk that remains alive over generations. The word translated "branches"

refers to the disciples themselves. It usually referred to the small, green tendrils that grew from year to year out of the long-lasting vine. Each year these tendrils had to be handled with care. Dead tendrils had to be removed. The ones that didn't produce fruit had to be pruned back so that fruitful ones could grow. Jesus isn't being subtle here—it would be ludicrous to think that a tendril could survive on its own for even a day without being connected to the main vine as its source of nourishment and strength. At the same time, the very reason the vine exists is to produce fruit, and the fruit only comes from the tendril branches. The vine and the branches are organically interconnected in a way that is essential if fruit is to be produced.

Jesus's point is that our most fundamental need as disciples is to stay constantly connected to him, to "remain in me." We never outgrow our need for Jesus because we never get to a place where we no longer need the forgiveness and righteousness that only he can provide. That sounds like a pretty basic fact, but it often gets lost in discipleship models. Yet it's a point made repeatedly throughout the New Testament: "So then, *just as you received* Christ Jesus as Lord, *continue to live* your lives in him, rooted and built up in him, strengthened in the faith as you were taught, and overflowing with thankfulness" (Colossians 2:6–7; emphasis mine).

Two enormous implications follow from Jesus's teaching that we need to have him—and the message of the gospel—central in our lives. The first is that fruit isn't something we produce on our own. Fruit is something Christ produces in us as we remain connected to and dependent on him. In John 15, the fruit Jesus has in mind is the sum total of what the gospel produces in us and through us. It includes prayer (v. 7), obedience (v. 10), joy (v. 11), our love for one another (v. 10–17), and our witness as we point others to Jesus (v. 26). This fruit comes as we receive, depend on, and live out of the love God has for us *as* we reach out to love others. It all depends on staying rooted in Christ in the same way that branches stay connected to the vine. I've often felt that it's up to me to produce fruit in my life and ministry. Jesus says it's just the opposite: my job as the branch is to stay connected to him, and his job as the vine is to produce the fruit through me.

The second major implication is that when we are disconnected from Jesus, we can accomplish nothing whatsoever. Again, Jesus uses the strongest possible language to communicate this. Unlike English, in Greek it is perfectly acceptable to have a double negative, but it is only used for the most emphatic way of saying "no." If I were to translate verse 5 literally, it would say, ". . . apart from me you cannot do nothing" or ". . . apart from me you can do **nothing** at all." Nothing. Zero. Zip. Zilch. Nada. No-thing.

At a heart level, I don't often read the verse that way. Too often I live as if Jesus is saying something more like, "Apart from me, you can do quite a bit, but when you get stuck, come back and get reconnected and I'll help you out." Jesus, however, means what he says. Apart from him we can do nothing to produce the spiritual fruit we are created to produce to glorify God.

Over the years, I've come to realize why my expectations for that first mission trip were so misplaced. I had expected the trip itself to change me, to somehow make me more spiritual. In reality, the trip showed me just how big my need is to stay constantly connected to Jesus. It's the staying-constantly-connected-to-Jesus-through-the-gospel that changes us, not the experience of a mission trip.

My hope is that you'll start to see the same thing over the next week or two. It's easy to forget how much we need Jesus. The truth is that I need him the same way I need air. In the hectic pace of normal life, it's easy to miss this. But when I go swimming and dive underwater, my need for air becomes immediately apparent—and urgent. In many ways a mission trip is like living underwater for a few weeks. It takes us out of our normal environment and shows us just how much we need to breathe in Jesus every minute. It shows us how much we need the good news of the gospel ourselves, even as we try to help others meet Jesus.

RESPONDING TO GOD *(15 Minutes)*

1. Look through the passage again and circle the word "remain" every time it appears. What do you think Jesus is trying to communicate about the importance of staying spiritually connected to him?

....

....

....

....

....

2. It's obvious that before we come to faith, the message we most need to hear is the gospel—the good news about all that Jesus is and all that Jesus has done. However, after we come to faith, it sometimes seems like we need to "move on" to something beyond the gospel: discipleship, spiritual disciplines, becoming more holy, etc. That understanding of the gospel looks something like this:

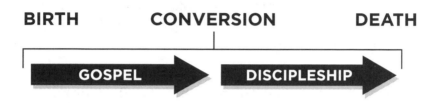

BIRTH   **CONVERSION**   **DEATH**

GOSPEL   DISCIPLESHIP

The truth, though, is that we never outgrow our need for Jesus, because we never get to the point where we can run our lives without him. In fact, a large part of spiritual maturity is growing in our ability to see how much we need Jesus every minute of every day, turning to him and depending on him, rather than ourselves, more and more.

And because we never outgrow our need for Jesus, we never outgrow our need for the grace of the gospel. Believing the gospel isn't just the way we begin the Christian life, it's also the way we continue to grow all through our Christian life. This understanding of the gospel looks something like this:

BIRTH   **CONVERSION**   **DEATH**

GOSPEL

What are some implications of thinking about the Christian life this way?

....

....

....

....

....

3. Where are you most tempted to rely on something other than Jesus
    to produce "fruit" in your life or ministry? What has happened when
    you've tried to do this?

....

....

....

....

....

Spend a few minutes asking Jesus to show you, over the course of the trip,
when you are putting your faith in something other than him and his good
news.

WHAT I SAW GOD DO TODAY . . .

This evening (or tomorrow morning), take a few minutes to record unique
ways that you saw God at work. Our sin-hardened hearts easily forget, so
writing down a few of the things you've seen God do is a great way to offer
thanks and praise to him.

Today I saw God . . .

....

....

....

....

....

JESUS IS THE ONE WHO SECURES YOUR IDENTITY

Date: ....

Location: ....

How I'll Be Serving Today:..

....

....

BIG IDEA

It's tempting to think that doing a good job on our trip or seeing lots of fruit from our work is what makes us "successful." But Jesus points out that no matter how well (or poorly!) our ministry is going, our relationship with him is what establishes our worth and identity. It is the foundation of our deepest joy.

MEETING WITH GOD *(15 Minutes)*
JESUS SENDS THE SEVENTY-TWO (LUKE 10:1–20)

[1]After this the Lord appointed seventy-two others and sent them two by two ahead of him to every town and place where he was about to go. [2] He told them, "The harvest is plentiful, but the workers are few. Ask the Lord of the harvest, therefore, to send out workers into his harvest field. [3] Go!

I am sending you out like lambs among wolves. [4] Do not take a purse or bag or sandals; and do not greet anyone on the road.

[5] "When you enter a house, first say, 'Peace to this house.' [6] If someone who promotes peace is there, your peace will rest on them; if not, it will return to you. [7] Stay there, eating and drinking whatever they give you, for the worker deserves his wages. Do not move around from house to house.

[8] "When you enter a town and are welcomed, eat what is offered to you. [9] Heal the sick who are there and tell them, 'The kingdom of God has come near to you.' [10] But when you enter a town and are not welcomed, go into its streets and say, [11] 'Even the dust of your town we wipe from our feet as a warning to you. Yet be sure of this: The kingdom of God has come near.' [12] I tell you, it will be more bearable on that day for Sodom than for that town.

[13] "Woe to you, Chorazin! Woe to you, Bethsaida! For if the miracles that were performed in you had been performed in Tyre and Sidon, they would have repented long ago, sitting in sackcloth and ashes. [14] But it will be more bearable for Tyre and Sidon at the judgment than for you. [15] And you, Capernaum, will you be lifted to the heavens? No, you will go down to Hades.

[16] "Whoever listens to you listens to me; whoever rejects you rejects me; but whoever rejects me rejects him who sent me."

[17] The seventy-two returned with joy and said, "Lord, even the demons submit to us in your name."

[18] He replied, "I saw Satan fall like lightning from heaven. [19] I have given you authority to trample on snakes and scorpions and to overcome all the power of the enemy; nothing will harm you. [20] However, do not rejoice that the spirits submit to you, but [continually] rejoice that your names are written in heaven."

THE BEST MISSION TRIP EVER!

Everyone wants to have a great mission trip, but it's hard to imagine things going any better than they did for the disciples in today's passage. It may have been the most perfect mission trip in history!

It was great because it was initiated directly by Jesus and open to those beyond his inner circle. Seventy-two new disciples are to go and prepare different areas for his arrival and further ministry (v. 1). Jesus instructs these disciples to trust God entirely for their provisions. His Father will meet all of their needs on the trip, even without their raising support or bringing supplies with them (vv. 2–8). Jesus also gives them power and authority to heal the sick as a way to announce that the Messiah's kingdom is near (v. 9). He publicly condemns anyone who does not welcome them or accept their message (vv. 10–16). And when it is all over, Jesus is full of joy and offers a prayer of thanksgiving over the group (vv. 21–24).

This amazing mission trip produced results that were absolutely astounding. In verse 17, we see that the seventy-two returned filled with joy. Because they were pursuing the mission Jesus gave them, and because of his authority and power, even demons submitted to them. In the poetic language of verse 18, Jesus describes Satan falling from heaven in the same way that lightning appears to fall from a great height to the earth. The reason for this is revealed in verse 19: Jesus has given his followers his own authority, power, and protection to overcome anything that would oppose his message, whether physical or spiritual.

As impressive as all of this is—and it *is* impressive—Jesus goes on to make an utterly shocking statement in verse 20: "However, do not rejoice that the spirits submit to you, but rejoice that your names are written in heaven." Despite everything that has been accomplished, Jesus does not want his disciples to lose sight of what is truly important. He knows that in our fallen hearts lurks the temptation to define ourselves by something other than our relationship with him. In verse 20, Jesus warns both his disciples and us not to rejoice in the success of ministry, but in the fact that we are known by the Father and that our place in his presence is secure. The verb tenses here indicate that this rejoicing over our names being written in heaven is to be continual, ongoing. It shouldn't rise and fall depending on how well our ministry is going. Likewise, when he says that our names "are written," he's using a very specific verb tense to let us know that although our names were written at one point in time, they will remain recorded forever. They won't fade away over time. Success in ministry may come and go, but our connection to Christ is permanent.

It's so easy for me to forget this. There are enough "sexy" false Jesuses out there—approval, control, success, self-generated righteousness—that my fallen heart is often tempted to define my worth by who I am and what

I do instead of by *whose* I am. Failures can easily discourage me and make God seem distant and disapproving. Successes whisper that "Patric the god" is doing just fine on his own. No need for daily repentance and faith here, thank you very much. The truth is that whenever something defines me other than the finished work of Christ—be it my greatest achievements or my worst failures—it's a sin. And as obvious as that seems, it's a lesson I'm still struggling to learn.

A few years ago, as part of a mission trip to central Europe, I was asked to teach about humility. I hadn't spoken on the subject before, so I was hesitant to take the assignment. I didn't think I would do a very good job. When I shared this with a teammate, he playfully responded that my lack of experience with humility was one reason they asked me to speak about it! I reluctantly agreed and started my preparation. But no matter how hard I tried, things just wouldn't come together. I wasn't sure how to apply what I was learning to other people's lives. I didn't know the culture well. My personal illustrations seemed too "American" for the audience. Plus I'd be working through a translator, which adds another level of complexity. Truthfully, if I could have gotten out of the assignment, I would have, because I just knew it wasn't going to go well. But I trudged on with my preparation, largely because backing out would have been even more embarrassing than teaching poorly.

On the morning I was supposed to teach, I took my pile of scribbled notes up to the front, prayed, and started teaching. Lo and behold, the most amazing thing happened. Everything came together! For the first time, I saw how to approach the subject in a way that would make sense for the audience. My translator and I got into a good rhythm. God brought to mind a few helpful illustrations. By the time I sat down, I had gone from fearful and discouraged to smugly pleased with myself. "Well, Patric, it turns out that you *are* a pretty good teacher after all. Knew it all along."

You can see the problem, can't you? My reactions—frustration, fear, and discouragement when things weren't going well, and independence and pride when they did—both have the same root cause. In each case, I was letting my performance determine my identity and my relationship with God. Instead of finding my worth, value, and security in Christ and what he has accomplished for me, I was looking to my teaching ability to establish my reputation. I was far more impressed with ministry success than with having a Father in heaven who knows my name and who is securely guiding my every step to bring me back home to his presence.

The reason Jesus's warning in verse 20 stands out so starkly is because it comes after wonderful ministry success. The disciples had been given a mandate, they followed it and obeyed, and their trip had gone amazingly well. Likewise, my talk about humility had finally come together. My teaching had been clear and effective. But as verse 20 reminds us, Jesus isn't fooled. He knows that we need to be saved from our successes every bit as much as we need to be saved from our sins. He understands better than we do how easy it is to get so enamored with "how things went" that we lose sight of "who we are." And whenever that happens, it means that we've lost sight of the cross—the only foundation able to hold us firmly in place as the winds of success and failure swirl around us.

RESPONDING TO GOD *(15 Minutes)*

As we grow spiritually, we begin to see how holy God really is and just how sinful, broken, and needy we are. Jesus, through his work on the cross, bridges that gap between God's holiness and our sinfulness. But when we allow our successes (in the form of religious performing) or our failures

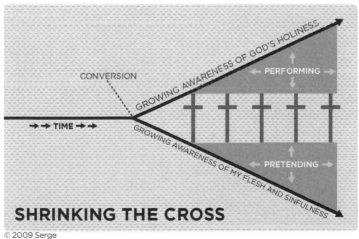

SHRINKING THE CROSS

© 2009 Serge

(in the form of spiritual pretending) to define our identity, we minimize Christ's work on the cross.

Take a look at the illustration above and then answer the following questions.

1. Yesterday we looked at ways we rely on things other than Jesus. When you think about the patterns of your everyday life, where are you most likely to rely on your successes (your performance) to create a sense of worth or value for yourself?

    ....

    ....

    ....

    ....

    ....

    Where have you seen that tendency already on the trip?

    ....

    ....

    ....

    ....

    ....

2. When you think about the patterns of your everyday life, where are you most likely to allow your failures (and the ways we tend to cover up our failures by "pretending" things are better than they are) to define your worth or value for yourself?

    ....

    ....

....

....

....

Where have you seen that tendency already on the trip?

....

....

....

....

3. In our passage today, Jesus tells us to rejoice more over the fact that our names are written in heaven than over "successful ministry." Take a few minutes to list some of the things Jesus has done for you that make you grateful to God. Use them throughout this week as spiritual reminders to keep looking to Christ.

    Example: Because of Christ's death on the cross, I'm now God's child. Even when I mess up, I know that God's love for me doesn't change, because of what Christ had done for me.

    First Truth:

    ....

    ....

    ....

    Second Truth:

    ....

    ....

    ....

Third Truth:

....

....

....

Throughout the rest of the trip, start looking for ways to remind yourself (and others) of these foundational truths of the gospel. When things go well, remind yourself of what Jesus offers you, which is more fulfilling than success or your spiritual performance. When things don't go well and you blow it, remind yourself that your failures don't define you. Jesus and his work does! Knowing this will give you the confidence to confess your sins and start over as you depend more deeply on him than on yourself!

WHAT I SAW GOD DO TODAY . . .

This evening (or tomorrow morning), take a few minutes to record unique ways that you saw God at work. Our sin-hardened hearts easily forget, so writing down a few of the things you've seen God do is a great way to offer thanks and praise to him.

Today I saw God . . .

....

....

....

....

....

JESUS IS THE ONE WHO EQUIPS YOU THROUGH HIS SPIRIT

Date: ....

Location: ....

How I'll Be Serving Today:...

....

....

BIG IDEA

Mission trips sometimes put us in seemingly impossible situations where we feel like we are in over our heads. But Jesus has promised to never leave us without protection or resources. The Holy Spirit lives in us to equip, empower, teach, and lead us, accomplishing God's will in and through us, even when we feel like we aren't up to the task.

MEETING WITH GOD *(15 Minutes)*

JESUS PROMISES THE HOLY SPIRIT (JOHN 14:15–27)

15 "If you love me, keep my commands. 16 And I will ask the Father, and he will give you another advocate to help you and be with you forever—

[17] the Spirit of truth. The world cannot accept him, because it neither sees him nor knows him. But you know him, for he lives with you and will be in you.

[18] "I will not leave you as orphans; I will come to you. [19] Before long, the world will not see me anymore, but you will see me. Because I live, you also will live. [20] On that day you will realize that I am in my Father, and you are in me, and I am in you. [21] Whoever has my commands and keeps them is the one who loves me. The one who loves me will be loved by my Father, and I too will love them and show myself to them."

[22] Then Judas (not Judas Iscariot) said, "But, Lord, why do you intend to show yourself to us and not to the world?"

[23] Jesus replied, "Anyone who loves me will obey my teaching. My Father will love them, and we will come to them and make our home with them. [24] Anyone who does not love me will not obey my teaching. These words you hear are not my own; they belong to the Father who sent me.

[25] "All this I have spoken while still with you. [26] But the Advocate, the Holy Spirit, whom the Father will send in my name, will teach you all things and will remind you of everything I have said to you. [27] Peace I leave with you; my peace I give you. I do not give to you as the world gives. Do not let your hearts be troubled and do not be afraid."

GOD ISN'T TOO WORRIED ABOUT YOUR INABILITY

"I nearly burst into tears. After all, what could we do? What could *I* do that would make any difference at all?"

Those were the words of a friend of mine, reflecting on a mission trip to help run a mobile medical clinic in rural Africa. Faced with daunting poverty and the lack of even basic healthcare, the situation could often feel hopeless, even for experienced team members.

In this case, a three-year-old girl had been brought in to be seen by the team. Malnutrition had left her stunted for her age; she was listless, covered with sores, and laboring for breath. Her family had abandoned her, assuming that she would die, but a kindly neighbor had carried her for several miles (with five children of her own in tow) to see if anything could be done. The nurses did what they could and asked the neighbor if she would be willing to return the next day for further treatment.

"We watched them leave and cried together," my friend said, recalling the episode. That night the team set aside additional supplies and clothes in case the little girl came back. "But I confess we didn't have much hope for that. We knew how sick she was. We knew that her family had given up hope and the neighbor had children of her own to look after. So we prayed, but without much faith."

Anyone who has ever been on a mission trip has seen and experienced things that make them feel overwhelmed and discouraged. But Jesus isn't limited by our inability, lack of resources, or even our small faith. He's more than able to accomplish the tasks he has called us to, even when we can't.

In our passage today, Jesus is spending one last night with his disciples before the horrifying events of his arrest, trial, and crucifixion. Earlier in the chapter (John 14:1–14), Jesus reassured and comforted his disciples that, although his departure was near, his leaving was necessary and for their benefit.

Jesus affirms to his disciples that he won't leave them as orphans, children who have to fend for themselves without the love, protection, and resources a family provides. But if Jesus is leaving, how will he provide for them? Jesus is going to ask God the Father to send God the Holy Spirit to be with them and to work in and through them.

This is an important point we often overlook: God the Father so loved the world that he not only sent his only begotten Son to save us, he also sent his Spirit of truth to ensure that his saving work in our lives and his work in the world would be brought to completion.

In this passage, Jesus describes the Holy Spirit as an advocate who will help us and stay with us forever (John 14:16). As the Spirit of truth (v. 16), he reminds us of what Christ has said and done so that the gospel will deepen in our lives (v. 25). A few chapters later, Christ tells the disciples that the Holy Spirit will bring about conviction of sin and lead his followers into truth (John 16:7–15).

Although they were both sent by the Father, Jesus and the Holy Spirit have unique ministries that are essential for our salvation and welfare. Christ took on human flesh and voluntarily restricted himself with a human nature, locating himself in human time and space. The Holy Spirit, however, remains entirely a spirit, so he is able to indwell all believers throughout the world and throughout history. This allows the message of the gospel to be taken effectively to every corner of the globe (see John 14:12). Christ has paid for our sins and given us his perfect record of obedience, while the Holy Spirit assures our hearts that we really have been forgiven and that we stand before the Father wrapped in Christ's righteousness. In Galatians 4:1–7, Paul reminds us that God the Father sent Christ to redeem us and make us his children (vv. 4–5). He also sends the Holy Spirit into our hearts to assure us that we really are loved by our heavenly Father and that we can trust and depend on him (v. 6). So Christ's promise to have the Father send the Holy Spirit is of huge importance. Christ is reminding his disciples, and us, that though he isn't physically present, God's power is. And that power—not our efforts or abilities—is what accomplishes his purposes in our lives and ministry.

For instance, when we struggle with sin and feel like there is no way God could use such big sinners, it is the Holy Spirit's job to remind us that we are perfect in the Father's eyes because of what Christ has done on the cross (Hebrews 10:14). When we feel like no one understands us, or that maybe God has forgotten us because we are struggling and suffering, the Spirit reminds us that we are God's adopted sons and daughters (Romans 8:14–16). When it is hard to pray, the Spirit reminds us that he is praying for us with such deep emotion that it can't even be expressed in human words (Romans 8:26–27). At every moment, we have the third person of the Trinity, the Holy Spirit, guiding, helping, comforting, praying, encouraging, and teaching us. Not only that, the Spirit is the one who enables those who don't know Christ to come to faith (John 3:5–8).

No part of our lives or ministry can be effective without the work of the Holy Spirit. Jesus understood that, so he offers his disciples the greatest comfort he can provide—a glimpse into the coming of the Holy Spirit and what that would mean for them and their calling.

You can imagine my friend's surprise, when against all odds, the neighbor did return with the sick little girl the next day. The team cleaned her up, tended to her sores again and gave her clean clothes. They found a trusted church member and gave her money for medicine and food for the girl. But once again the situation seemed desperate. What were the odds that this would all turn out well? Fortunately our inability is no hindrance to God's ability to work through us.

"We were weak. We had little faith. But God . . . . He did something more amazing than we could have asked or imagined," my friend confessed. That little girl? She's twelve years old now, living with a church family that took her in and continued the good work that began on that hard day, so many years ago. Reflecting on that experience, my friend noted, "We weren't up to the task of helping this little girl. But God was. Through us, through the neighbor, through the church, and now through her new family, God was able to do what we couldn't."

It's the same for you and me. We tend to assume that it's up to us produce results on our trip. But Jesus reminds us that God provides both the plan *and* the power to accomplish his purposes. He, not us, is the Great Physician who is mending his creation one soul at a time. And through the power of the Holy Spirit he is able to use our limited, weak efforts to accomplish things we never imagined. Our job is to listen and respond in faith, even when it seems impossible.

RESPONDING TO GOD *(15 Minutes)*

Learning to listen to God and depend on his Holy Spirit to work through us takes some intentionality on our part. The following "Five Minute Drill" is a way to learn how to do this. It's something you can do anytime, anywhere. Work through the following explanation and exercise now, and then look for ways to use it today and throughout the rest of the trip.

NOTICE WHEN YOU'RE FEELING OUT OF SORTS
(1 minute)

Pay attention to any time you feel overwhelmed, out of control, anxious, frustrated, scared, like you are all alone, etc. These are usually signs that something isn't right in your heart and that God would like to talk with you about something.

In the last day or two, where have you felt "out of sorts" emotionally or spiritually?

....

....

....

....

....

> *Example:* I just got assigned to the door-to-door evangelism team for the day and I'm feeling a lot of anxiety about that.

ASK THE HOLY SPIRIT TO REVEAL YOUR UNBELIEF
(1 minute)

Even if you are keeping calm on the surface, whenever you notice that you're feeling unsettled, spend a minute or two asking the Holy Spirit to reveal what is going on in your heart. Often it's caused by our unbelief—there is something about the gospel or about Christ that we are not receiving, trusting, or relying on.

> *Holy Spirit,* what am I not believing is true about God, his love for me, and his provision for me?

....

....

....

....

....

> *Example:* I think the reason I am so anxious is that I am afraid I will look foolish, or that the people who answer the door will

immediately reject me. I don't like being in situations where I'm not in control, and I'm feeling like God has left me all alone in this.

LISTEN FOR THE HOLY SPIRIT TO REMIND YOU OF THE GOSPEL *(2 minutes)*

Once the Holy Spirit has helped you identify where you may not be believing the gospel, ask him to help you see how God is able to meet your needs. Scripture, the words of a worship song, and spending time recounting God's promises or past answers to prayer are all great ways to be reminded of the truth of the gospel.

> *Holy Spirit,* now that I'm starting to see what I'm not believing about God, remind me what is true, based on God's Word.

....

....

....

....

....

> *Example:* In light of my anxiety, I need to cling to God's promises.

- I'm not alone; God is always with me and he's always in control (Isaiah 41:10).
- God's power is perfected in my weakness (2 Corinthians 12:9).
- I'm here to love others because Jesus has first loved me (1 John 4:9–12).
- It's okay if I look foolish because my reputation is established by Christ's work on the cross, not by what I do or fail to do (Philippians 3:8–9).

REENGAGE THE SITUATION *(1 minute)*

Now that you've had a little "gospel sanity" restored, it's time to reengage the situation. Remember that no matter what the task is, God is right there with you. He wants to partner with you to accomplish his work. He's the "senior partner" and you're the "junior partner," so you can always look to him for his leading when you aren't sure what to do.

How does God want to partner with me in order to see my trust and dependence on him grow, as we do the work at hand?

....

....

....

....

....

> *Example:* Okay, I'm going to knock on a door and when I do, I'm going to trust that my Father is in charge, that he loves the people who live there (even if I'm scared of them!), and that he wants to work in and through my fear to connect with them.

This process is a helpful way to be sensitive throughout the day, encouraging us to be continually aware of and dependent on the Holy Spirit. It's more about changing your mind-set than about adding more "to do's" to your list. And because it's not about "measuring up spiritually" but rather about "being more aware of the needs we already have," it allows our needs to drive us back to Christ. We'll check back in on this process later in the week to see how things are going.

WHAT I SAW GOD DO TODAY . . .

This evening (or tomorrow morning), take a few minutes to record unique ways that you saw God at work. Our sin-hardened hearts easily forget, so writing down a few of the things you've seen God do is a great way to offer thanks and praise to him.

Today I saw God . . .

....

....

....

....

....

JESUS IS THE ONE WHO MOTIVATES YOU TO LOVE OTHERS

Date: ....

Location: ....

How I'll Be Serving Today:...

....

....

BIG IDEA

When we try to serve others out of duty or a desire to make ourselves look good, we aren't really loving Jesus or others. However, when we can see how great our sin is and how lavishly Jesus has met our needs, gratitude and forgiveness will lead us to love Jesus and others.

MEETING WITH GOD *(15 Minutes)*

JESUS ANOINTED BY A SINFUL WOMAN (LUKE 7:36–50; NIV)

[36] When one of the Pharisees invited Jesus to have dinner with him, he went to the Pharisee's house and reclined at the table. [37] A woman in that

town who lived a sinful life learned that Jesus was eating at the Pharisee's house, so she came there with an alabaster jar of perfume. [38] As she stood behind him at his feet weeping, she began to wet his feet with her [many] tears. Then she [kept wiping] them with her hair, kissed them and poured perfume on them.

[39]When the Pharisee who had invited him saw this, he said to himself, "If this man were a prophet, he would know who is touching him and what kind of woman she is—that she is a sinner."

[40]Jesus answered him, "Simon, I have something to tell you."

"Tell me, teacher," he said.

[41]"Two people owed money to a certain moneylender. One owed him five hundred denarii, and the other fifty. [42]Neither of them had the money to pay him back, so he forgave [canceled] the debts of both. Now which of them will love him more?"

[43]Simon replied, "I suppose the one who had the bigger debt forgiven."

"You have judged correctly," Jesus said.

[44]Then he turned toward the woman and said to Simon, "Do you see this woman? I came into your house. You did not give me any water for my feet, but she wet my feet with her tears and wiped them with her hair. [45]You did not give me a kiss, but this woman, from the time I entered, has not stopped kissing my feet. [46]You did not put oil on my head, but she has poured perfume on my feet. [47]Therefore, I tell you, her many sins have been forgiven—as her great love has shown. But whoever who has been forgiven little loves little."

[48]Then Jesus said to her, "Your sins are forgiven."

[49]The other guests began to say among themselves, "Who is this who even forgives sins?"

[50]Jesus said to the woman, "Your faith has saved you; go in peace."

HOW HAD THINGS GONE SO HORRIBLY AWRY?

It's easy to forget that we need Jesus just as much as the people we have come to serve. Even after twenty-five years, I still remember the day I started to realize this.

Every afternoon on this particular mission trip, our team would spread out with a short survey about spiritual subjects. We'd ask strangers if they'd be willing to share their thoughts with us. The hope was that some would be ready for a deeper spiritual conversation and we'd get to share the gospel with them. In reality, though, this almost never happened, which, oddly enough, was okay with me. I'd assumed that the real point of the assignment was to complete as many surveys as possible in the allotted time—which I did, with relish. I took real pride in always completing more surveys than anyone else. The rest of the team was made up of committed, spiritually mature people and, despite my youth, I wanted to show everyone how truly dedicated I was.

Imagine my shock when one afternoon a kindly older woman gladly took the survey and then invited me to tell her more about Christ. She was engaged and spiritually open. It was by far the best evangelism I had ever done. Everything was going perfectly—until I glanced at my watch and realized that I'd spent the entire two-hour window speaking with this one woman. My heart panicked. "Oh no, Patric! You're only going to have one survey to turn in today. What are people going to think about you?" I had barely finished this thought when another popped into my mind. "Of course, if this woman actually accepts Christ right now, that would be even *better* than having a load of completed surveys, wouldn't it?"

What followed was one of the worst things I've ever done as a follower of Jesus. I invited her to give her life to Christ. But when she said that she wasn't quite ready, I pressed more forcefully. She resisted. I pushed harder. Finally, knowing that my time was up and that I'd have only one survey to show for my effort, I stood up, looked her in the eye and said, "Well, if you want to go to hell, I guess that's your problem, isn't it?"

Yes, I really said that.

What happened? How had things gone so horribly awry?

Since that day, I have come to see that I was not really on that trip to love people who didn't yet know Jesus. I was there to do my duty as a "spiritually mature Christian." And doing my duty—by completing more surveys than everyone else—was my way of generating my own sense of righteousness and establishing my reputation with the rest of the team. It's a deadly combination, one that Jesus encountered many times.

In our passage today, Jesus is invited to dinner by a Pharisee named Simon so that Simon and his friends could check Jesus out. But someone far more controversial than Jesus shows up as well—a woman known to be squarely outside the bounds of acceptable society.

By telling us that she had led a "sinful life," Luke is saying that the woman had been sexually promiscuous and had probably accepted money or gifts in return for sexual favors. Yet here she is, braving the looks of contempt and indignant mutterings of the religiously righteous, entering Simon's house to see Jesus. It's what she did when she finally met Jesus, though, that was truly shocking.

Following the custom of the time, the guests would have been seated, semi-reclined on low couches arranged in a horseshoe or U-shape. As guest of honor, Jesus would have been seated next to Simon on the short end of the rectangle—the "head" of the table. When the woman, disdained by most of the men as a prostitute, finds Jesus, she comes and stands behind him. Everyone would have been able to see her and Jesus clearly from their couches.

As she stands there, the woman is overwhelmed with emotion and starts weeping. She cries so much that her tears begin to wet Jesus's feet. Noticing that Simon hadn't asked a servant to clean Jesus's dusty, filth-covered feet, she does the unthinkable. She takes down her hair and begins to clean and dry Jesus's feet with it! In those days, a Jewish woman's hair was considered her crowning glory. It was always worn up, or covered, and only let down in private in the presence of her husband. Taking her hair down and using it in this way demonstrates just how much she loves Jesus and cares for him. Afterwards, she takes what is likely the most expensive thing she has ever owned—an alabaster jar containing the best perfume money can buy. Typically this would have been reserved for her dowry or her own or a loved one's burial. Instead, she uses it to anoint Jesus's feet. Those who have been forgiven much love much. They love with their whole hearts and they willingly give their best.

This is too much for Simon. As a Pharisee who prided himself on his strict obedience to God's law, he is too self-contained to explode in public. Jesus, nevertheless, can see into Simon's heart. In response to Simon's judgmental thoughts, Jesus tells a story about two men who have debts cancelled; then he links it to the events that have just unfolded. The woman offered Jesus lavish expressions of her faith, love, and gratitude for his willingness to forgive her sins. In contrast, Simon hadn't even offered his "guest of honor" the most basic expressions of hospitality. Because Simon's sins weren't known publicly and the woman's were, Simon thinks that she's the big sinner in the room. But Jesus didn't see things that way at all. Simon's religious pride and self-reliance, which led to a lack of love for Jesus, are just as sinful as the woman's public promiscuity. In fact, between Simon and the woman, only the woman can see just how much she needs Christ's forgiveness and salvation. Simon thinks he's doing just fine on his own.

This woman's actions are a stunning picture of coming to Jesus in faith. She illustrates what it looks like to love and serve God in response to his forgiveness and redemption. She also demonstrates what it looks like to follow Jesus wholeheartedly—to live missionally. She comes into a place where she is neither welcome nor understood, and she lines up behind Jesus so that nobody can see her without first seeing him. She then kneels behind Jesus, her only hope, and weeps as a broken sinner while intimately, personally, and lavishly pouring out her tears and her possessions for the One who has changed her life.

Just like me all those years ago, Simon, with his sense of religious duty, is spectacularly ill-equipped to see his own sin. Simon doesn't love Jesus, because Simon doesn't see just how much he needs the mercy and forgiveness that only Christ can give. The woman, on the other hand, could see her own sin clearly enough to know that Jesus is the only one who could ever meet her need for cleansing and forgiveness. She received his love and forgiveness and, in receiving them, she begins to selflessly love him in return.

There is a danger on every mission trip. It's the danger that we, like Simon, will ignore or minimize our sin and in so doing end up ignoring and minimizing the radical forgiveness and love that Jesus offers us. When that happens, our love for God and for others disappears pretty quickly. The truth is that we are never going to be very good at taking the gospel to others if we secretly think they need it more than we do.

RESPONDING TO GOD *(15 Minutes)*

Take some time to talk with God as you work through the following questions. Be as honest as you can. After all, God already knows what's going on in your heart and he still loves you endlessly.

Writing down some of your answers will help you see how God has been at work in your life and in others. Feel free to use abbreviations or "code" if you refer to specific people or events.

1. When have you served like Simon (serving out of duty and loving very superficially) this week? When have you served like the woman (serving out of gratitude and loving others sacrificially) this week?

....

....

....

....

....

2. What was different when you were serving people out of duty vs. serving them out of love? Do you think the people you were serving could tell the difference?

....

....

....

....

....

3. The woman in our passage was motivated to love Jesus out of gratitude for the forgiveness he offered. Spend a few minutes thinking about all

of the blessings you have as a result of being "in Christ." These include things like:

- Having every single one of your sins paid for by Christ on the cross.
- Having all of Christ's righteousness credited to you.
- Being brought into God's family as a beloved son or daughter.

Blessings that are mine in Christ . . .

....

....

....

....

....

The power to serve others in hard situations doesn't come from simply gritting our teeth and dutifully getting through it. Like the sinful woman in the passage, love begins by first having our hearts melted by what Jesus has done for us. But love never stops with just "Jesus and me." Jesus always invites us to love others in response to the ways he's first loved us.

Be on the lookout this week for times when you are tempted to serve like Simon (i.e., simply doing your religious duty instead of wholeheartedly loving someone) and be ready to recall some of the blessings you've listed above. When you are struggling to love others, ask God to help you recall the blessings you have in Christ and change your attitude. You may want to review your list (above) mentally several times during the day.

WHAT I SAW GOD DO TODAY . . .

This evening (or tomorrow morning), take a few minutes to record unique ways that you saw God at work. Our sin-hardened hearts easily forget, so writing down a few of the things you've seen God do is a great way to offer thanks and praise to him.

Today I saw God . . .

....

....

....

....

....

JESUS IS THE ONE WHO SHOWS YOU HOW TO LAY DOWN YOUR LIFE

Date: ....

Location: ....

How I'll Be Serving Today:..

....

....

BIG IDEA

Living and serving alongside fellow sinners can reveal hidden sins lurking in our hearts—pride, selfishness, and a desire to get our own way—which often lead to conflict and strife. But Jesus, the ultimate Servant, has a different paradigm in mind for us—humility, dying to self, and serving others.

MEETING WITH GOD *(15 Minutes)*
JESUS WASHES HIS DISCIPLES' FEET (JOHN 13:1–17, LUKE 22:24–27²)

(John 13:1) It was just before the Passover Festival. Jesus knew [was very aware] that the hour had come for him to leave this world and go to the Father. Having loved his own who were in the world, he loved them to the end.

² The evening meal was in progress, and the devil had already prompted Judas, the son of Simon Iscariot, to betray Jesus. (Luke 22:24) A dispute also arose among them as to which of them was considered to be greatest. (John 13:3) ³ Jesus knew that the Father had put all things under his power, and that he had come from God and was returning to God; ⁴ [in light of this,] he got up from the meal, took off his outer clothing, and wrapped a towel around his waist. ⁵ After that, he poured water into a basin and began to wash his disciples' feet, drying them with the towel that was wrapped around him.

⁶ He came to Simon Peter, who said to him, "Lord, are you going to wash my feet?"

⁷ Jesus replied, "You do not realize now what I am doing, but later you will understand."

⁸ "No!" said Peter, "You shall never [by no means ever] wash my feet." Jesus answered, "Unless I wash you, you have no part with me."

⁹ "Then, Lord," Simon Peter replied, "not just my feet but my hands and my head as well!"

¹⁰ Jesus answered, "Those who have already had a bath [been bathed] need only to wash their feet; their whole body is [remains] clean. And you are clean, though not every one of you." ¹¹ For he knew who was going to betray him, and that was why he said not every one was clean.

(Luke 22:25) Jesus said to them, "The kings of the Gentiles lord it over them; and those who exercise authority over them call themselves Benefactors. ²⁶ But you are not to be like that. Instead, the greatest among you should be like the youngest, and the one who rules like the one who serves. ²⁷ For

---

2. Although the Gospel narratives do not explicitly order the timeline of events during the Last Supper, commentators agree that the disciples' argument about who was the greatest took place *before* Jesus washed their feet. I've put the events in the order that seems to make most sense out of the separate events in John's account and Luke's account, though it is possible that the entire argument and response by Jesus in Luke 22 took place before Jesus washed the disciples' feet in John 13.

who is greater, the one who is at the table or the one who serves? Is it not the one who is at the table? But I am among you as one who serves."

(John 13:12) When he had finished washing their feet, he put on his clothes and returned to his place. "Do you understand what I have done for you?" he asked them. ¹³ "You call me 'Teacher' and 'Lord,' and rightly so, for that is what I am. ¹⁴ Now that I, your Lord and Teacher, have washed your feet, you also should wash one another's feet. ¹⁵ I have set you an example that you should do as I have done for you. ¹⁶ Very truly I tell you, no servant is greater than his master, nor is a messenger greater than the one who sent him. ¹⁷ Now that you know these things, you will be blessed if you do them."

THESE PEOPLE ARE DRIVING ME CRAZY!

A Serge missionary once quipped that going into missions is like "pouring Miracle-Gro® on your sins." Truer words have never been spoken!

Mission trips have a way of wearing through the veneer of politeness and self-sufficiency that most of us rely on at home. Not only are we battling a new environment, a new schedule, and often a new culture, we face all of our ordinary struggles too. External processors get seated next to internal processors on long plane, train, and car rides. Early risers become room-mates with night owls, and at least one person snores. Those who prefer to travel light end up having to help lug the bags of folks who bring everything but the kitchen sink. On top of that, we're all thrown together in a sort of spiritual cage match, unable to retreat to the peace and safety of "home" the way we normally can. Add in a few long days of ministry and it's easy to see how conflict, hurt feelings, and resentment are part of every mission trip.

But the realities of mission trips do something else too. They reveal something that was there all along—the hunger in our hearts for things only Jesus can give.

In our passages today, Jesus is nearing the end of his earthly ministry. John 13 and Luke 22 record some of the last moments Jesus will have with his disciples before his arrest and crucifixion. But what was supposed to be a final, intimate gathering of spiritual brothers has deteriorated into bicker-ing about reputations and rights; a return to a frequent squabble about who should serve and who should be served. In a very real sense, the disciples were saying through their actions and arguments, "I may not be perfect, but I'm better than you."

Of course, there was someone in the room who *was* actually perfect and who *did* deserve to be served by everyone else. What was Jesus's response to all of this? A stern rebuke? An exasperated appeal for the disciples to get their act together? No. Instead, the master becomes a servant, so that his sinful creatures can see their need for a Savior.

As twenty-first century readers, it's easy for us to miss what would have been obvious to the original audience. First, only the most lowly servant, often only non-Jewish slaves, would be assigned the task of foot washing. It was a humbling task that no one would perform unless he was forced to do so. Yet Jesus again confounds everyone's expectations, assuming the role of slave to show his sin-stunted disciples just how great God's love for them truly was.

Second, even if Jesus took only a few minutes with each disciple, it would have likely taken thirty to forty minutes to serve everyone. And every disciple—including Judas!—would have watched as Jesus repeated the process over and over again until it was their turn. What would you be thinking as Jesus, your Lord and Master, the Son of God who is your Savior, the one who had raised people from the dead and cast out demons, knelt down before you, looked you lovingly in the eyes and took your dirty, smelly feet in his hands to wash them?

Peter is the only one with enough nerve to say what everyone else was probably thinking. "Really Jesus? *You* are going to wash *my* feet? I can't have that!" But Jesus knows exactly what is at stake, and it's far more than dirty feet or jockeying for position. The disciples still haven't understood what it's going to take to ultimately cleanse them from their sins. So Jesus insists. And, of course, Peter resists. John's language helps us understand that Peter's opposition is real: "No, Jesus. You will never, *ever*, under any circumstances wash my feet." But Jesus is just as emphatic. Without the sacrificial cleansing that Jesus would soon accomplish for him on the cross, Peter—and the rest of us—would remain mired in sin. No amount of self-generated achievement will be enough to give us the record we need to stand before God. What started out as disagreement about "who was the greatest" has come full circle: How can anyone, ever, be accepted by a holy God, no matter how "great" we are? Jesus knew that over the next few hours, his disciples would find out exactly what it would take to not just become acceptable, but to be welcomed by the Father as beloved sons.

It's shocking to me that Jesus washed Judas's feet right along with everyone else's. If one of my teammates had betrayed me with the hope of seeing me put to death, I wouldn't go out of my way to love him. Yet the ugliness of Judas's betrayal, the blindness of Peter's pride, the disciples' bickering about their status, or my grumbling about carrying someone's extra luggage all have a common cause. They are all the result of failing to see that Jesus—and *only* Jesus—is enough to satisfy our deepest needs.

I'd like to think that I'm a lot more spiritually perceptive than the disciples. But most of the time, I'm not. I'm too preoccupied with my place, position, status, and reputation. I too want to be served, which leads to the same sort of grumbling conflict that the disciples had on that night so long ago.

But it doesn't have to be that way. The gospel offers a different way to live and love others that is open to me, even when it's hard or I don't feel like it.

When my heart gets anxious or frustrated at not being treated the way I think I deserve, the gospel reminds me to look to the One who truly loves me. In those moments, my deepest need isn't just for more patience or humility, though I need those things too. My deepest need is to be cleansed from a heart that wants achievement and reputation to establish my worth and identity. In Christ, I have all that I need and he welcomes me to come and be satisfied in him. Jesus never tells me to suck it up and serve my teammates. Instead he serves me. Through his coming, dying, and rising again, Jesus gives me what I could never earn for myself. Then he invites, commands, and enables me to receive *his* power and *his* grace, the only things that can free me to love and serve others. Even when they snore.

RESPONDING TO GOD (15 Minutes)

Take some time to talk with God as you work through the following questions. Be as honest as you can. After all, God already knows what's going on in your heart and he still loves you endlessly.

Writing down some of your answers will help you see how God has been at work in your life and in other lives. Feel free to use abbreviations or "code" if you refer to specific people or events.

1. Where has this trip "poured Miracle-Gro®" on your sins so far? What are the specific ways you have been having conflict with people over the last few days? (Reminder: Even if you've bitten your tongue or covered up your inner feelings, God is interested in dealing with your heart.)

....

....

....

....

....

2. In our passages today, we see that the disciples' hearts were hungry for honor and recognition. They all desired to be served in some way instead of being the ones doing the serving. When you have been frustrated with others this week, what are the things you think your heart has been hungry for?

....

....

....

....

....

3. In serving his disciples by washing their feet, Jesus is making two points. First, their unwillingness to wash each other's feet reveals how much they need the cleansing that only he can bring through his death on the cross. Second, because he has served them so generously—giving

up his life so that they can be cleansed and made right with God—he is calling them to serve others in the same way. Spend a few minutes thinking through the challenges you've had loving others and complete the following journaling exercise:

Jesus, like your disciples, I would rather have things my own way, to be served rather than to serve. Where are you calling me to die to self and love people in deeper ways?

....

....

....

....

....

Jesus, will you help me see how I need you more deeply than I think I do? Show me what is holding me back today from loving and serving others the way you want me to.

....

....

....

....

....

Friend, Savior, Redeemer, remind me now of one or two key truths about who you are and what you have done for me so that I can rely on them today to love other people better. (List them below.)

• ....

....

....

• ....

....

....

• ....

....

....

Whenever I'm feeling frustrated or fed up with others, help me to look to you and listen for your voice as you remind me of these truths throughout the day.

WHAT I SAW GOD DO TODAY . . .

This evening (or tomorrow morning), take a few minutes to record unique ways that you saw God at work. Our sin-hardened hearts easily forget, so writing down a few of the things you've seen God do is a great way to offer thanks and praise to him.

Today I saw God . . .

....

....

....

....

....

DEVOTIONAL

JESUS IS THE ONE WHO PROVIDES FOR YOUR EVERY NEED

Date: ....

Location: ....

How I'll Be Serving Today: ....

....

....

BIG IDEA

When we rely on our own strengths, abilities, and resources, we won't have what it takes to do the things that Jesus is calling us to do. But when we understand that we aren't up to the task and turn instead to Christ in faith, he will always provide more than we need.

MEETING WITH GOD *(15 Minutes)*

JESUS FEEDS THE FIVE THOUSAND (JOHN 6:1–15; NIV)

[1]Some time after this, Jesus crossed to the far shore of the Sea of Galilee (that is, the Sea of Tiberias), [2]and a great crowd of people followed him because they saw the signs he had [regularly] performed by healing the sick.

58

³Then Jesus went up on a mountainside and sat down with his disciples. ⁴The Jewish Passover Festival was near.

⁵When Jesus looked up and saw a great crowd coming toward him, he said to Philip, "Where shall we buy bread for these people to eat?" ⁶He asked this only to test him, for he already had in mind what he was going to do.

⁷Philip answered him, "It would take more than a half year's wages to buy enough bread for each one to have a bite!"

⁸Another of his disciples, Andrew, Simon Peter's brother, spoke up, ⁹"Here is a boy with five small barley loaves and two small fish, but how far will they go among so many?"

¹⁰Jesus said, "Have the people sit down." There was plenty of grass in that place, and they sat down (about five thousand men were there). ¹¹Jesus then took the loaves, gave thanks, and distributed to those who were seated as much as they wanted. He did the same with the fish.

¹²When they had all had enough to eat, he said to his disciples, "Gather the pieces that are left over. Let nothing be wasted." ¹³So they gathered them and filled twelve baskets with the pieces of the five barley loaves left over by those who had eaten.

¹⁴After the people saw the [miraculous] sign that Jesus performed, they began to say, "Surely this is the Prophet who is to come into the world." ¹⁵Jesus, knowing that they intended to come and make him king by force, withdrew again to a mountain by himself.

THIS IS NOT WHAT I SIGNED UP FOR

I remember when I hit the wall on a mission trip. I think it was the lettuce that did it. I'm not sure, but they probably washed the lettuce in the tap water I had been so diligently avoiding. The result? A sleepless night spent traipsing back and forth between the poorly ventilated room I was sharing with six other guys and the only available bathroom three floors below. As the sun was coming up, in my jet lag exhaustion, I remember thinking, "This is *not* what I signed up for. I didn't raise all this money and come all this way to be exhausted, sick, and stuck with a bunch of smelly guys."

It's not always as grim as that, but no mission trip ever goes as planned. There are so many opportunities for things to go wrong. There is lost luggage and missed connections. The supplies you need for your project didn't arrive or aren't quite what you need. Folks that you like a lot back home end up getting on your nerves. Or you are simply overwhelmed by the deep needs of the people you came to serve. You may be working at a mobile medical clinic, bringing healthcare to those who can't get to the nearest town, and you're overwhelmed by the poverty and disease you see.

You're there to make a difference, to get things done, to be useful. And instead you feel overwhelmed, stretched, and taxed. Things are not turning out the way you expected. What should you do? What *can* you do?

It's okay. Jesus has plenty of experience dealing with frustrated and anxious hearts. Our passage today is a reminder that whenever we are called to do God's work, Jesus will always show up to provide exactly what we need to do it.

Leading up to the events in today's passage, Jesus and the disciples had been in a pretty intensive season of ministry. Jesus had sent them out in pairs on a short-term mission trip to preach and heal (Mark 6:1–13). After reuniting, word of John the Baptist's execution reaches them (Matthew 14:12–13). But despite their sorrow, ministry didn't slow down at all. In fact, there were so many demands on their time that the disciples didn't even have time to eat! So Jesus invites them to get away with him for some much-needed rest (Mark 6:30–31). And that's when things really start to get out of hand.

A crowd of 5000 men, plus their families, tracks Jesus down and is quickly approaching. Jesus doesn't seem fazed at all. He already knew what the crowd needed and what his disciples needed. The crowd needed bread; the disciples needed faith. So instead of jumping into action, he turns to Philip and asks, "Where shall we buy bread for these people to eat?" As John points out, there is more to Jesus's question than meets the eye.

In a sense, Jesus is offering Philip a very clear choice: "Philip, in light of the overwhelming situation we are facing, what are *you* going to do to meet everyone's needs?" The text doesn't tell us how Jesus asked the question, but it's not hard to imagine him having a bit of a twinkle in his eye. After all, the Creator of the sun, moon, and stars is standing right there. Surely coming up with a little bread isn't going to be a problem.

But Philip's response, much like my own, doesn't offer a solution. It only highlights the impossibility of the situation. That's because Philip, much like me, looks to himself instead of looking to Jesus to provide. Jesus knows that the crowd's hunger, Philip's finances, and Andrew's offer of some tiny barley loaves and a dab of fish aren't the issue. The issue is faith. Who are the disciples going to look to when the needs are real and the provisions are woefully inadequate?

Jesus is the only one who can see clearly that, more than bread, fish, money, solitude, or rest, what the disciples need most is him. He is their sustainer and provider. He alone can meet the needs of the crowd. He is their comfort and rest. In order to help them see what they had been missing, Jesus calmly tells his disciples to have everyone sit down. (I wish I could have seen the look on Philip's face when Jesus said that!)

Then something quite miraculous happens. Bread and fish start being given out—to everyone. What was completely impossible for the disciples—feeding the entire crowd—is no problem at all for Jesus. God's provision for the things he calls us to do is always abundant when we look to him in faith, when we trust him instead of relying on our own strengths, plans, abilities, and provisions. There is so much food that, when it's all said and done, there are twelve baskets of bread left over. Jesus's provision is lavish and generous. It's never skimpy or barely enough.

And where does this leave the disciples? Once they start to rely on Jesus's provision instead of their own strength to meet people's needs, they are given a high privilege indeed. They get to see God at work up close. They get to be a conduit of God's grace as they pass out the bread. They get to see people fed and transformed. They get to see the difference between knowing that Jesus *could* provide, and experiencing his grace as he *does* provide. I'm not sure what Philip thought he was signing up for that day, but I'll bet he got more than he bargained for.

RESPONDING TO GOD *(15 Minutes)*

Take some time to talk with God as you work through the following questions. Be as honest as you can. After all, God already knows what's going on in your heart and he still loves you endlessly.

Writing down some of your answers will help you see how God has been at work in your life and in others' lives. Feel free to use abbreviations or "code" if you refer to specific people or events.

1. Where have I been relying on my own strengths, abilities, or resources during our trip in order to do ministry? How has that been working out?

....

....

....

....

....

2. Where have I seen God provide for me (or our team) in unexpected ways over the last several days? Remember: God provides for you as well as through you. See if you can list a few examples of each.

....

....

....

....

....

3. How has God provided through you today?

....

....

....

....

....

4. Where are you still struggling to believe that God will generously pro-
    vide for you? It may be in relation to this trip or it could have something
    to do with your life back home too.

....

....

....

....

....

> *Jesus,* when I think about how capable you are to meet, supply,
> and provide for my every need, and how often I still look to
> myself or outside resources, I want to tell you . . .

WHAT I SAW GOD DO TODAY . . .

This evening (or tomorrow morning), take a few minutes to record unique
ways that you saw God at work. Our sin-hardened hearts easily forget, so
recording a few of the things you've seen God do is a great way to offer
thanks and praise to him.

Today I saw God . . .

....

....

....

....

....

JESUS IS THE ONE WHO WELCOMES YOU BACK AFTER YOU'VE MESSED UP

Date: ....

Location: ....

How I'll Be Serving Today: ....

....

....

BIG IDEA

No matter how hard we try to be perfect, none of us are, this side of heaven. Learning to return quickly to Jesus when we sin, knowing that he'll always welcome us back home, is the key to keeping our spiritual and personal relationships healthy.

MEETING WITH GOD *(15 Minutes)*

THE PARABLE OF TWO LOST SONS (LUKE 15: 1-2; 11-32)

[1] Now the tax collectors and sinners were all gathering around to hear Jesus. [2] But the Pharisees and the teachers of the law muttered, "This man welcomes sinners and eats with them."

[11] Jesus continued: "There was a man who had two sons. [12] The younger one said to his father, 'Father, give me my share of the estate.' So he divided his property between them.

[13] "Not long after that, the younger son got together all he had, set off for a distant country and there squandered his wealth in wild living. [14] After he had spent everything, there was a severe famine in that whole country, and he began to be in need. [15] So he went and hired himself out to a citizen of that country, who sent him to his fields to feed pigs. [16] He longed to fill his stomach with the pods that the pigs were eating, but no one gave him anything.

[17] "When he came to his senses, he said, 'How many of my father's hired servants have food to spare, and here I am starving to death! [18] I will set out and go back to my father and say to him: Father, I have sinned against heaven and against you. [19] I am no longer worthy to be called your son; make me like one of your hired servants.' [20] So he got up and went to his father.

"But while he was still a long way off, his father saw him and was filled with compassion for him; he ran to his son, threw his arms around him and kissed him.

[21] "The son said to him, 'Father, I have sinned against heaven and against you. I am no longer worthy to be called your son.'

[22] "But the father said to his servants, 'Quick! Bring the best robe and put it on him. Put a ring on his finger and sandals on his feet. [23] Bring the fattened calf and kill it. Let's have a feast and celebrate. [24] For this son of mine was dead and is alive again; he was lost and is found.' So they began to celebrate.

[25] "Meanwhile, the older son was in the field. When he came near the house, he heard music and dancing. [26] So he called one of the servants and asked him what was going on. [27] 'Your brother has come,' he replied, 'and your father has killed the fattened calf because he has him back safe and sound.'

²⁸ "The older brother became angry and refused to go in. So his father went out and pleaded with him. ²⁹ But he answered his father, 'Look! All these years I've been slaving for you and never disobeyed your orders. Yet you never gave me even a young goat so I could celebrate with my friends. ³⁰ But when this son of yours who has squandered your property with prostitutes comes home, you kill the fattened calf for him!' ³¹ 'My son,' the father said, 'you are always with me, and everything I have is yours. ³² But we had to celebrate and be glad, because this brother of yours was dead and is alive again; he was lost and is found.'"

THE IMPORTANCE OF A GOOD RECOVERY

I'm not the handiest guy in the world when it comes to home improvement projects. So it was with some trepidation that I agreed to serve on our missions trip construction crew. My first assignment seemed simple enough: remove the faucet in the old kitchen so that we could replace the sink. If you've ever done this, you know that the only way to loosen the nuts and bolts that hold the faucet in place is to twist yourself under the sink and work above your head with very little clearance. Despite my best efforts for almost forty minutes, I could not get the nuts to budge, no matter how hard I tried. Finally, embarrassed and frustrated, I asked another guy to help me. He got under the sink, took a look around, fiddled with the wrench and took the bolts off in about two minutes. Astounded at his progress, I asked what the secret was. He smiled at me sheepishly and said, "You were tightening them instead of loosening them." Evidently in all my contortions I got my "lefty loosey, righty tighty" mixed up.

Repentance is a bit like that. As long as I was turning the nut in the wrong direction, it was going to remain stuck. I needed a complete reversal of direction to see progress. Our spiritual lives echo this. When we are heading down the path of unbelief, no matter how sincere we are or how hard we are working, we're going in the wrong direction. In his book, *Keep in Step with the Spirit*, J. I. Packer provides a great definition of repentance when he says, "Repentance means turning from as much as you know of your sin, to give as much as you know of yourself, to as much as you know of your God, and as our knowledge grows at these three points, so our practice of repentance has to be enlarged."[3] We can see those dynamics at play in our passage for today.

Jesus has been getting complaints from the Pharisees and teachers of the law that he is spending too much time with the worst of the worst. In response, he tells three interconnected parables, the last of which is about two brothers and their relationship with their father. There is amazing richness in this story, but for our purposes, I want to highlight three things.

First, both of the brothers are lost. Even though the younger brother gets the lion's share of the attention, the older brother is just as alienated from his father, as his responses in verses 28–30 indicate. It is just as easy to be lost in duty and obligation as it is be lost in rebellion. Though we don't often think of it this way, we need to repent of our good deeds as much as we do of our sins, when those good deeds have led us to think self-righteously that God owes us something.

Second, the father generously welcomes both sons back. Because the younger son has disgraced his father and the rest of the family, his welcome must be public and lavish, lest he be seen as a second-class citizen for the rest of his days. In the parable, the father does what no self-respecting Jewish father would ever do in real life: seeing his son in the distance, he gathers up his robes and raises them above his knees so that he can run to his son. When he gets there he literally "falls upon his neck" and kisses him tenderly. He then lavishly and publicly welcomes him home with new clothes, the family ring, and a party. Likewise, when the older brother shames his father by refusing to attend the party for his brother, the father again does the unexpected. He leaves the party and pleads with his older son. In each case, the father willingly takes on the shame and humiliation his sons had caused through their behavior in order to restore their relationship.

Finally, even the most incomplete repentance overjoys the father. Although the younger son begins to come to his senses, it's clear that he isn't really returning home with a broken heart over what he has done to his family and the pain he has caused his father. Instead, he plans to make some sort

3. J. I. Packer, *Keep in Step with the Spirit: Finding Fullness in Our Walk With God* (Grand Rapids: Baker Books, 2005 rev. edition), 87.

of formal apology to get a little food (vv. 17–18). But before the son can utter a single word, the father has run to him, embraced him, and welcomed him. Repentance is the door to joy and reconciliation, even when it's done imperfectly.

Growing in our ability to repent is an essential part of spiritual growth because our need for it is so pervasive. For instance, even if I only sin five times a day (a wildly optimistic notion!), and I don't count all my sins of failing to do something I should have done (a completely unjustified omission), at this point in my life I've committed well over 80,000 sins—and counting. Given that, the importance of repentance cannot be underestimated. Every day we live on earth, until Christ comes back or we die, we will wrestle, struggle, and often fall into sin. Repentance isn't an occasional act. It, along with faith, is a lifestyle to be embraced. As in the parable, it's also the path back to peace and joy with our heavenly Father.

Yet most of the time I don't really see repentance as something joyful. Just like asking for help to remove the kitchen faucet, I tend to see repentance as a sort of sad necessity. I pursue it, but only as a last resort. But because repentance is so closely tied to faith, and our need for faith is daily and ongoing, so is our need for repentance. Repentance is what frees us to joyfully receive all that Christ has for us, so that we can depend on him with trusting hearts. Repentance is what enables us to enjoy our Father's embrace and experience his steadfast mercy.

RESPONDING TO GOD (15 Minutes)

Repentance and faith are not just how we begin our relationship with Jesus. They are also fundamental ways that we continue to grow in our relationship with Jesus. For our repentance and faith to deepen, we need to see not just the surface sin (i.e. the fruit sin) but also what is causing it (i.e. the root sin).

Take some time to talk with God as you work through the following questions. Be as honest as you can. After all, God already knows what's going on in your heart and he still loves you endlessly.

1. Think of a time in the last twenty-four hours when you've blown it. It may be something you thought or said, the way you treated someone, or an attitude of unbelief you've come to see in your own heart.

   - What happened?

   ....

   ....

   ....

   ....

   ....

   Example: When we were getting ready to go to the work site, Janice said to me, "Hurry up, slowpoke, or we'll all be late."

   - What was the surface sin in your example?

   ....

   ....

   ....

   ....

   ....

   Example: Janice's critical comment really made me mad at her. I didn't lose my temper or say something nasty to her, but I was really hurt by her comment, so I froze her out for the rest of the day. I refused to make eye contact and walked away whenever I saw her coming. The surface sin was being angry with Janice and the way I froze her out.

- What was the deeper sin? What was really causing the surface sin to happen?

....

....

....

....

....

Example: I was angry with Janice because I felt judged by her. She was attacking my reputation by suggesting that I'm always late. Ultimately I was angry because I want to be approved by others instead of getting my approval from Jesus. That was the root sin, wanting to be approved by others instead of resting in the approval I already have in Christ. When her approval was taken away, I got angry and froze Janice out.

2. Growing in repentance means learning to repent not just of our surface sins, but also of the sinful roots that produce our sinful actions. In the example above, I didn't (outwardly) lose my temper with Janice or say something mean to her, but I still sinned. I sinned by being angry with her in my heart (surface sin). I also sinned by rejecting God as my ultimate source of identity and approval, as I tried to satisfy that need by seeking the approval of others (deeper/root sin).

- What would it have looked like for you to repent of the surface sin you listed above?

....

....

....

....

Example: I would have needed to recognize that I was angry with Janice and ask God to show me why, instead of expressing my anger by ignoring her and freezing her out. I may need to ask Janice if she noticed my actions. If she did, I'll need to ask her how my anger impacted her. Regardless of what she did, I still responded wrongly.

- What would it have looked like for you to repent of the deeper sin you listed above?

....

....

....

....

....

Example: Before I talked with Janice, I would have asked God to break my heart, not just over the anger, but over the fact that I make people's approval into an idol—something I can't live without. In essence, when Janice "stole" my idol by denying me approval, I murdered her in my heart with my anger. Even though I knew I shouldn't be mad, I was. So I tried to punish her, but in ways that didn't make me look bad.

As you finish up your time with God today, spend some time asking him to show you where a lack of repentance is blocking your relationship with him or others. You can use the "prayer starter" language below or come up with your own.

Holy Spirit, I don't want to be the kind of person that stays mired in sin or repents superficially. Will you show me where I am doing that, so that I can turn from it as quickly as I can and return as quickly as I can to you? What key promise from your Word would you like me to hang on to as I go about my day?

WHAT I SAW GOD DO TODAY . . .

This evening (or tomorrow morning), take a few minutes to record unique ways that you saw God at work. Our sin-hardened hearts easily forget, so recording a few of the things you've seen God do is a great way to offer thanks and praise to him.

Today I saw God . . .

....

....

....

....

....

DEVOTIONAL

JESUS IS THE ONE WHO WALKS WITH YOU IN UNCERTAINTY

Date: ....

Location: ....

How I'll Be Serving Today:..

....

....

BIG IDEA

Most of us like to think that we're in control of our lives and that by being strong and focused we can meet our own needs. But when the illusion of our control or strength is shattered, Jesus is always there to remind us that he is the one truly in control and we can completely cast ourselves on him.

MEETING WITH GOD *(15 Minutes)*

JESUS CALMS THE STORM (MARK 6:45–52; NIV)

⁴⁵ Immediately [As soon as the meal was finished] Jesus made his disciples get into the boat and go on ahead of him to Bethsaida, while he dismissed the crowd. ⁴⁶ After leaving them, he went up on a mountainside to pray.

⁴⁷Later that night, the boat was in the middle of the lake, and he was alone on land. ⁴⁸He saw the disciples straining at the oars, because the wind was against them. Shortly before dawn, he went out to them, walking on the lake. He was about to pass by them, ⁴⁹but when they saw him walking on the lake, they thought he was a ghost. They cried out, ⁵⁰because they all saw him and were terrified.

Immediately he spoke to them and said, "Take courage! It is I. Don't be [Stop being] afraid." ⁵¹Then he climbed into the boat with them, and the wind died down. They were completely amazed, ⁵²for they had not understood about [what Jesus had done with] the loaves; their hearts were hardened [still calloused by unbelief].

THE TRAIN IN SPAIN STAYS MAINLY IN THE . . .

The scene: a train platform in Spain.

The characters: A short-term mission team with thirty Americans and an entire platform full of very curious Spaniards.

The problem: Trying to load thirty people and their gear onto a crowded train in under two minutes.

The result: A train leaving the station with half of our team still standing on the platform.

My response: Well, let's just say that the twelve disciples had nothing on me when it comes to doubting that Jesus knows what he is doing.

I'm not sure who thought it was possible to actually get all of us and our gear onto the train in two minutes. But somewhere along the line, a travel agent, a Eurail representative, or an overly optimistic schedule planner thought it could be done. So there we were, standing on the platform as half of our team and luggage started pulling out of the station. By this time we had attracted quite an audience of curious onlookers, some of whom were cheering us on, some of whom were mocking, and some of whom were just hoping that the clueless Americans weren't going to screw up their own travel plans.

As the train began to leave, in desperation our team leader called us together, told us to hold hands, bow our heads, and start praying. A hush fell over the crowd on the platform . . . until the titters of laughter started. I vividly remember standing there holding hands, feeling humiliated, bowing my head and thinking, "Are you kidding me?! Praying isn't going to help. We need to figure out how to actually get *on* the train instead of wasting time praying."

A lot has changed in my life since that afternoon. But one thing hasn't. I'm still pretty terrified of being utterly dependent on Jesus. Even when I look back on all that God has done in my life, and the ways he has provided time and time again, I often struggle to believe that he is bigger than my circumstances. And I'm not alone.

In the verses before our passage, Jesus has just finished feeding 5000 hungry men, plus their wives and children, with the contents of a little boy's lunch pail (see John 6:9). Having participated in that miracle, you'd think that Jesus's disciples would have been a little further along in understanding that Jesus is able to meet and exceed all of their needs. But turning self-reliant spiritual orphans into trusting sons is not the work of a single meal—even when that meal was expressly designed to show them their Father's love, provision, and trustworthiness.

As today's story unfolds, it's clear that Jesus is being very intentional about helping his disciples see their unbelief. First, he insists that the disciples get in the boat without him. Then Jesus spends several hours alone praying, insuring that his friends will be placed in a difficult and frightening situation as the storm pushes in. Finally he comes to them, but even then the disciples—ravaged by the wind and spiritually blinded by their unbelief—fail to see Jesus for who he really is and instead think he is a ghost. Jesus is nothing if not determined to put us in places where our own efforts and resources are insufficient. He wasn't unaware of his friends' circumstances or trials as they struggled in the storm. He was consciously putting them in a place where reliance on him was the only thing they could do, because he knew that the lesson from the feeding of the 5000—that he loves them and will not abandon them to their own resources—still hadn't sunk in (see v. 52). Jesus knows far better than we do that we will always instinctively choose to rely on our own strengths, gifts, and resources.

I can readily relate to the disciples' complete astonishment when Jesus showed up in such an amazing way. Because as we were bowing our heads and praying on that train platform in Spain—and as I was silently mired in my unbelief—the train . . . stopped. A gracious rail official had seen our plight, stopped the train, brought porters to help us reload our luggage in a baggage car, and upgraded us all to first class. If you could have compared the look on my face to the look on the disciples' faces that stormy night, they would have been identical. We all were absolutely, completely astounded that our circumstances were not bigger than God, that he was not ignoring us or abandoning us, but rather was giving us (again!) the best gift a Father can give: rest that comes from relying and depending on him instead of ourselves.

I've still got a long way to go, but slowly I've started to understand that dependence is not the harsh requirement of a stern and distant Father, as my heart so often supposes. It is actually one of the great gifts God gives us. Dependence is his way of helping us see that his love, goodness, and care for us are absolute—far more solid than the wispy illusions we so often cling to. Dependence is a challenge because it reveals how little we believe that God is enough, and how often we look to something other than him to make us secure, happy, safe, or fulfilled. The Bible has a word for those things: idols.

As you go about serving today, regardless of the challenges, difficulties, or disappointments, you don't go alone. Jesus is right there with you. Jesus was perfectly able to meet his own needs but nevertheless trusted our Father so completely that he volunteered to be dependent, even to the point of dying the cross. No matter where you go or what you face, you have a Friend who understands, who can help, and who is right there with you.

RESPONDING TO GOD *(15 Minutes)*

Take some time to talk with God as you work through the following questions. Be as honest as you can. After all, God already knows what's going on in your heart and he still loves you endlessly.

Writing down some of your answers will help you see how God has been at work in your life and in other lives. Feel free to use abbreviations or "code" if you refer to specific people or events.

1. So far on the trip, where have you been struggling to believe that God is bigger than your circumstances? Try to identify a specific situation where it's been hard to depend on God over the last few days.

....

....

....

....

....

2. In the situations where you've wrestled with being dependent, what have you failed to believe about Jesus? What is objectively true about him that doesn't feel very real to you? (If you are having a hard time thinking of answers, review some of your favorite promises from Scripture).

....

....

....

....

....

3. Think back through today's passage and the previous devotional (John 6). Jesus abundantly provided for his followers in many ways. Use the following chart to identify some of the ways God has been providing for you and your team so far on this trip. When you are done, use the prayer prompt below to spend time praising God for what he has been doing.

Jesus Provided for the Disciples by . . .	Jesus Has Provided for Me/Our Team by . . .
(Physical needs)	(Physical needs)
(Safety)	(Safety)
(Working through their ministry)	(Working through our ministry)
(Spiritual comfort)	(Spiritual comfort)

Jesus, when I see how consistently you meet my needs in ways I could have never expected, I want to tell you . . .

WHAT I SAW GOD DO TODAY . . .

This evening (or tomorrow morning), take a few minutes to record unique ways that you saw God at work. Our sin-hardened hearts easily forget, so recording a few of the things you've seen God do is a great way to offer thanks and praise to him.

Today I saw God . . .

> *Note:* You may have already answered this when you filled out the chart in Question 3. But if you haven't, take a few minutes now to reflect on how God has provided for you today.

....

....

....

....

....

JESUS IS THE ONE WHO CARRIES YOUR BURDENS

Date: ....

Location: ....

How I'll Be Serving Today: ....

....

....

BIG IDEA

Loving God and loving others can feel like a huge burden, especially when we are already under the stress and strain of a mission trip. Jesus reminds us that he's eager to carry our burdens and encourages us to constantly turn to him to find true rest.

MEETING WITH GOD *(15 Minutes)*

JESUS INVITES US TO COME TO HIM (MATTHEW 11:27–30; NIV)

[Jesus prayed] ²⁷ "All things have been committed [handed over] to me by my Father. No one knows the Son except the Father, and no one knows the Father except the Son and those to whom the Son chooses to reveal him.

[28] "Come to me, all you who are weary and burdened, and I will give you rest. [29] Take my yoke upon you [on your shoulders] and learn from me, for I am gentle and humble in heart, and you will find [the deepest] rest for your souls. [30] For my yoke is easy [kind] and my burden is light."

WHEN REST DOESN'T LOOK LIKE REST

Sooner or later, everybody struggles on a mission trip. Whether it's the exhausting pace of hard work on a construction project, the noise and chaos of a developing world city, or the boundless energy that the kids at VBS or an English camp have, sooner or later we all get worn down. Add to that some frustration that the host culture simply doesn't "do things right," or feeling overwhelmed by the huge needs you see all around, knowing that you simply don't have the resources to help everyone. Finally, mix in a few nights with minimal sleep, strange food, and some team conflict and you've got a sure-fire recipe for everyone feeling on edge and stressed out.

In this context, loving other people well—our teammates, our ministry partners, and the nationals you came to serve—can feel like a huge burden. And yet Jesus still calls us to love one another with our whole hearts (Mark 12:31; John 13:34–35). So what do we do when we feel like things are too much to take? Where do we turn when the needs feel overwhelming and our ability to love others and meet their needs seems nonexistent?

In today's passage, Jesus talks about the things that weigh us down and wear us out. The religious leaders of his time were famous for the burdens they placed on people. They insisted on the rigorous observance of thousands of laws (many of which went beyond Scripture) through sheer willpower and human effort. It's not that obedience wasn't important to God—Jesus actually ups the ante by insisting that our external obedience flow from our internal love for God. But when human expectations define obedience instead of God's Word, and we rely on human effort to fuel that obedience, we become weighed down in ways God never intended.

So Jesus makes a startling invitation: Everyone who knows he is worn out and carrying too heavy a load is welcome to come to him and he will give him rest. The only requirement is to recognize our need and to be willing to come to him and take on his "yoke"—his way of obeying the Father.

To find the rest our souls so desperately need, we have to go about things differently. We can't rely on our own power and strength to please God and love others.

As most of Jesus's listeners would have known, a yoke was a wooden harness that eased the burden of carrying heavy loads or pulling a plow. Often teams of animals were "yoked" together to keep them pulling in the same direction. But it's most likely that in this case, Jesus has in mind a single yoke, the kind that enabled people to carry a heavy burden by spreading the weight across their shoulders. Nobody looked forward to wearing a yoke. It meant that a hard task was at hand. As soon as the load reached its destination, the yoke would immediately be thrown off. But, if a burden had to be borne, it was far better to do it with a yoke than without. For those who found the burden of pleasing God through self-effort and religious obedience too heavy, Jesus offered a different type of labor and a different type of yoke.

So just what kind of yoke is Jesus offering us? It's normally translated as being an "easy yoke" but in fact, Jesus uses a relational word to describe it. It is literally a "kind yoke." How can something that is imposed on us to carry a burden be kind? It's kind because it belongs to a kind master, who knows our frailty and has already stepped in to carry the heaviest load in our place. He continues to walk with us in our struggles.

Likewise, Jesus describes his burden as being light. I have to admit, at first glance, that idea strikes me as a little odd. After all, how can a "light burden" provide the "rest for my soul" that I so desperately need? When I hear the promise of having "the deepest rest for your soul," I tend to think of Jesus saying something like, "You poor dear. You've had it really rough, haven't you? Come sit down in my spiritual easy chair and have a nice long rest. You don't need to do anything anymore." But the rest Jesus promises doesn't come that way.

The rest Jesus promises isn't the result of inactivity or withdrawal. It comes from doing what God calls us to do (love him and love others) the way he calls us to do it (by relying on Christ's work and being empowered by the Holy Spirit). Jesus's burden is light, not because it removes the need for obedience, but because he has already carried it for us on the yoke of the cross. Jesus now offers his followers a different way of relating to God that enables us to truly love others instead of using them or being only superficially nice. It is this freedom—from putting ourselves first, from thinking we need to meet our own deepest need because we are spiritual orphans, from relying on our own strength to obey—that provides the deep rest our souls need.

But Jesus isn't merely giving me an invitation to rest. He is giving me something far greater: an invitation to **himself**. "Come to *me* . . . and *I* will give you rest." It is by coming to Jesus, abiding with him, that my soul finds the rest it so desperately craves, even when the situation seems impossible. Jesus doesn't ask us for more effort or ability, but to surrender to his kind yoke and light burden. This may feel like death at the time, but it is the only thing that frees us to receive all the riches Jesus offers, including his perfect restorative rest.

RESPONDING TO GOD *(15 Minutes)*

Back in Devotional 3, we introduced the idea of the Five-Minute Drill. Its purpose was to remind us to listen to God throughout the day so that we could intentionally rely on the Holy Spirit to work in us (i.e. show us our sin and apply the gospel to our hearts) and then to work through us (i.e., to allow us to reengage with people/situations, knowing that God is the "senior partner" who can use us to accomplish his purpose).

The Five-Minute Drill *consisted of:*

- Noticing when you're feeling out of sorts (1 minute)
- Asking the Holy Spirit to reveal your unbelief (1 minute)
- Listening for the Holy Spirit to remind you of the gospel (2 minutes)
- Reengaging the situation (1 minute)

If you're unsure about what each step involves, look back at pp. 37–40 to remind yourself.

1. What has your experience with the Five-Minute Drill been like so far?
    Were there parts that worked really well for you? Were there parts that
    were a struggle?

    ....

    ....

    ....

    ....

    ....

2. Think back through your week and identify a situation or two where
    you used the Five-Minute Drill. Then answer the following questions.
    (Don't worry if you haven't been consistent; just choose something
    you're currently struggling with.)

    •   What type of unbelief did the Five-Minute Drill help you uncover?
    Where did it help you to see patterns of unbelief in your life?

    ....

    ....

    ....

    ....

    ....

    •   As you listened for the Holy Spirit to remind you of the gospel,
    what did you hear?

    ....

    ....

    ....

....

....

- How did being reminded of your need for Christ, and his love for you seen on the cross, make a difference for you?

....

....

....

....

....

3. One of the best things about an exercise like the Five-Minute Drill is that it allows our *desperation* to bring about what our *discipline* rarely does—an ongoing, prayerful dialogue with God so that we can love others better. Our sin, our need, our brokenness all point us back to Christ and what he has done for us.

As you think about going back to "normal life" at home, spend a few minutes capturing some things you've learned about staying connected to Jesus and coming to him for rest in the midst of busy days and challenging situations.

....

....

....

....

....

WHAT I SAW GOD DO TODAY . . .

This evening (or tomorrow morning), take a few minutes to record unique ways that you saw God at work. Our sin-hardened hearts easily forget, so recording a few of the things you've seen God do is a great way to offer thanks and praise to him.

Today I saw God . . .

....

....

....

....

....

DEVOTIONAL

JESUS IS THE ONE WHO CHANGES THE WAY YOU SEE OTHERS

Date: ....

Location: ....

How I'll Be Serving Today: ....

....

....

BIG IDEA

It's easy to look at ourselves, our teammates, and those we serve and never see them the way God does. Jesus, however, can give us spiritual eyes to see ourselves and others as he does, which changes the way we love and engage with people to help introduce them to Christ.

MEETING WITH GOD *(15 Minutes)*
JESUS HEALS A LEPER (MARK 1:40-45)

[40] A man with leprosy came to him and begged him on his knees, "If you are willing, you can make me clean."

⁴¹ Jesus was filled with compassion. He reached out his hand and touched the man. "I am willing," he said. "Be clean!" ⁴² Immediately the leprosy left him and he was cleansed.

⁴³ Jesus sent him away at once with a strong warning: ⁴⁴ "See that you don't tell this to anyone. But go, show yourself to the priest and offer the sacrifices that Moses commanded for your cleansing, as a testimony to them." ⁴⁵ Instead he went out and began to talk freely [preach a lot], spreading the news. As a result, Jesus could no longer enter a town openly but stayed outside in lonely places. Yet the people still came to him from everywhere.

DO YOU SEE WHAT I SEE?

In many ways, the story of my spiritual life has been learning that most of what I thought was true really wasn't true at all. Assumptions I had about others, about myself, about who God is and what he wants have all undergone some pretty radical transformations over the thirty years I've been following Christ. A consistent catalyst in this process has been the mission trips I've taken. Through them I've discovered that I'm not the spiritual superhero I thought I was. I have experienced the beauty of grace and the jagged scars of sin in unexpected ways, in my life and in the lives of my teammates. I have discovered that God was far more generous and loving than I gave him credit for, and that his love for the world was far greater and more passionate than I ever could have imagined docked in the safe harbor of middle-class America. In many ways, mission trips have taught me to see life differently.

Our passage for today is also about changing the way we see things. In Mark 1, we meet a man afflicted with leprosy, a painful, disfiguring skin disease that, left untreated, is often fatal. In those days, it was assumed that the man contracted the disease as just punishment from God for committing a grave sin. Since leprosy was contagious and (at the time) incurable, the afflicted were forced to leave family and friends to live alone or with other lepers. They were also considered spiritually unclean and thus unable to participate in worship at the temple or synagogue. Imagine being afflicted with a painful, disfiguring, progressive disease and then being cut off from your loved ones and barred from church! It was horrible.

The man's leprosy is a physical representation of sin's effect on all of our lives. Sin causes physical suffering, it isolates us from those we love, and ultimately it separates us from God. And often when people see sin in our lives, they are only too willing to pass judgment on us. Sin also distorts the way we see God.

Try imagining the scene. A man, dying and disfigured, cut off from family, friends, and God, breaks all social and religious taboos by seeking out Jesus. He is desperate to be made clean. Whatever pride or self-sufficiency he once had is long gone, so he gets on his knees and begs the young rabbi for help. But because he has been so crushed by his circumstances, his view of God is warped. He is unsure if God even loves him anymore. Notice what he says: "If you are willing . . . ." *If*. He isn't doubting Jesus's power to heal him, but he's unsure if the Messiah is willing to be good to him personally, to care about *his* needs, given what he is. It is a heartbreaking scene that testifies to the devastating impact of sin and brokenness in our lives.

We live in a world that assumes that what we see on the surface is all there is. But Jesus sees much more. He sees the true needs of our souls and the intentions of our hearts. He sees the desperate ways we cling to things besides him. He knows what will truly heal and fulfill us.

Jesus's response to the leper invites us to see both the leper and Jesus differently. As Jesus looks down to see this wreck of a human who no longer knows if God cares about him, Mark says that Jesus wells up, overflowing with compassion. What must it have been like for the leper, so used to seeing people look away in horror, to look up into the eyes of the Alpha and Omega and see compassion and tenderness? Jesus then does something that hadn't happened for many years—he reaches out and touches the man, demonstrating his compassion with actions. Finally Jesus removes all doubt about his desire and ability to heal sin-ravaged people by saying, "I am willing. Be clean!" At that, this dead man walking among the living is brought back to health, life, and peace with God. Jesus doesn't see a desperate situation that is beyond hope. He sees a beloved son, needing to be welcomed home again.

Jesus's healing also changes the way the crowd sees the leper. No longer is the focus on his all-consuming identity as a leper. Instead he is sent to the priests to give thanks to God as a testimony to the Messiah's power and goodness. Cleansed and healed, the man rejects the minimal response outlined by Jesus. He went out and literally "preached a lot" about what Jesus had done for him. This would have major ramifications for Jesus. In the space of a few short verses, Jesus and the leper exchange places, foreshadowing the future exchange that Jesus would make with all sinners. Jesus, who was once at the center of the crowds, free to preach and do what he liked, is now confined to the lonely places because of the leper's preaching. The leper, once a solitary outcast, now moves freely around others, pointing them to Christ.

Mission trips also have the power to help us see ourselves and God differently.

- We come to realize that we aren't the strong, good people we assumed we were. We're broken and needy, fallen and finite, but still able to be used by God.
- Taken out of our daily routines where wealth and comfort dull our spiritual senses, we reawaken to how powerful God truly is and how much we need him every minute of our lives.
- Faced with overwhelming need, impossible opportunity, and open and hostile spiritual opposition, prayer once more starts to feel essential and powerful.
- As we encounter unexpected obstacles and opportunities, the myth of "having things under control" is unmasked for the illusion it is. Control belongs to God alone.

Ultimately I hope that you—for the first time or in a deeper way—have come to see that the gospel needed by the not-yet-Christians you have come to reach is the same gospel that's needed in your own heart. The people you have come to love and serve are not merely good people trapped in hard circumstances who need a little help. They are fellow sinners, whose sin is no less deep and no less present than our own. And their deepest need—though it may look drastically different on the surface—is no different than ours: The need for a Savior who not only says, "I am willing" but "It is finished," so that they too can be welcomed home as sons and daughters of the King.

RESPONDING TO GOD *(15 Minutes)*

As you finish your trip, take a few minutes to reflect on the questions below and on what God has done.

1. How do you see yourself, your teammates, and those you came to serve differently now than you did at the beginning of the trip?

    *   Yourself

    ....

    ....

    ....

    ....

    ....

    *   Teammates

    ....

    ....

    ....

    ....

    ....

    *   Those you came to serve

    ....

    ....

    ....

    ....

    ....

2. Like the leper, we all struggle at times, knowing that God is able to bring change and healing to our lives, but unsure if he is really willing to do so. How has this struggle played out for you on this trip, positively or negatively? Cite specific examples if you can.

....

....

....

....

....

3. The leper's response of telling others about Jesus was the overflow of a grateful heart. What are some examples of God's grace in your life for which you are grateful during the last ten days?

....

....

....

....

....

Jesus, I want to thank you for the way I've seen and experienced your grace during my time away. Is there anyone who doesn't yet know you that you want me to pursue when I return home? Help me to know how to love this person in your name.

AS YOU RETURN HOME

One of the most important parts of your trip happens after you return home. Once you've unpacked, set aside some time to reflect on what you saw God do in and through you and your team. *On Mission* includes three debrief exercises designed to help you do this and to make concrete plans for how to continue living on mission in your everyday life.

Right now, take a few minutes to skim through pages 116–134. Then turn to page 116 and set a date for completing *Debrief One: Making Sense of What You've Seen*. Ideally this exercise should be done on your journey home or within a week of your return. That way, all of the memories and experiences will be fresh in your mind.

WHAT I SAW GOD DO TODAY . . .

This evening (or tomorrow morning), take a few minutes to record unique ways that you saw God at work. Our sin-hardened hearts easily forget, so recording a few of the things you've seen God do is a great way to offer thanks and praise to him.

Today I saw God . . .

....

....

....

....

....

ADDITIONAL DEVOTIONAL RESOURCE
Introducing *Lectio Divina*[4]

Not every mission trip fits neatly into ten days. For those who will be doing a longer trip or simply want a change of pace from the standard devotions, I recommend that you try your hand at something called *lectio divina*.

Lectio divina (literally "divine reading") is a devotional way of reading Scripture that dates back to at least the twelfth century. It *slowly* approaches the biblical text in a way that helps us to really *hear* what it's saying, to *personalize* the text to our unique situations, to respond to God in *prayer*, and to *live* out the text. Many times we read Scripture too fast and superficially; we need to slow down. *Lectio divina* can be compared to enjoying a nourishing three-course meal at your favorite restaurant instead of speeding through a meal from a fast-food place.

There are four parts to this way of approaching Scripture.

1. *Lectio*: The slow reading of the text. As you approach the Scripture passage, take time to read it aloud (or silently to yourself). Treat the text as a letter directly written to you. Reflect on what you have read; don't rush. Listen to the gentle whisper of God speaking to you (1 Kings 19:12). Read it through two or three times, spending some time in silence between readings. Read until you find a particular word, phrase, or theme that captures your attention. This could be a word of comfort *or* disruption.

2. *Meditatio*: Meditating on the text. Here you focus on the particular words, phrase, or theme that stood out in your reading. This meditating is pondering or ruminating on one particular part of the text. Repeat to yourself the portion of text; perhaps even memorize it. As you meditate on it,

---

4. This introduction to *lectio divina* is adapted from *Gospel Growth: Becoming a Faith-Filled Person*, by Serge. To order copies of this study or other Serge::Resources materials, visit our publisher, New Growth Press: http://stores.newgrowthpress.com.

how does it speak to you—to your hopes, fears, or desires? What thoughts or memories come to mind? What is God saying to you this moment, on this day? What is God telling you about himself, about yourself, about your situation, or about people you know?

3. *Oratio:* Praying the text. The passage now serves as the basis for a conversation with your Father. Talk to him about what's on your heart and what your meditation has brought to your attention. Your prayer is now your response to God, based on what you have read and meditated. This may include thanks, questions, frustrations, praise, requests, or confession of sin.

4. *Contemplatio:* Putting the text into practice. Although this word sounds passive, this step emphasizes putting the text into action. We must now live the passage. This may be described as restful activity! It is living before God and enjoying his presence. Here you take what you have read, meditated, and prayed, and now go and live it. This is the full reception of the text, the incarnation of the text in your life—living it before God.

USING *LECTIO DIVINA*

To use the *lectio divina* devotional reading process, simply choose a passage of Scripture and work through each of the steps listed above. You don't need to go in order; some days you may spend more time in one or two elements of the process than you do in others.

It helps to choose just a few verses rather than a longer passage, so that you can really sit with each verse. As much as you can, slow down. Rest. Think. Absorb. And talk with God as you do.

LECTIO DIVINA READING ONE

Date: ....

Location: ....

Passage: ....

1. *Lectio:* Slowly read the text two or three times.
What words, phrases, or ideas capture your attention?

....

....

....

....

....

2. *Meditatio:* Meditate on the text.
What is God saying to you through these verses? What is he inviting you to? What assurance is he giving you?

....

....

....

....

....

3. *Oratio:* Pray the text.

What do you need to say to God in light of what you hear him saying to you in the passage?

....

....

....

....

....

4. *Contemplatio:* Put the text into practice.

As you think about your day, what is God calling you to?

....

....

....

....

....

LECTIO DIVINA READING TWO

Date: ....

Location: ....

Passage: ....

1. *Lectio:* Slowly read the text two or three times.

What words, phrases, or ideas capture your attention?

....

....

....

....

....

2. *Meditatio:* Meditate on the text.

What is God saying to you through these verses? What is he inviting you to? What assurance is he giving you?

....

....

....

....

....

3. *Oratio:* Pray the text.

What do you need to say to God in light of what you hear him saying to you in the passage?

....

....

....

....

....

4. *Contemplatio*: Put the text into practice.

As you think about your day, what is God calling you to?

....

....

....

....

LECTIO DIVINA READING THREE

Date: ....

Location: ....

Passage: ....

1. *Lectio*: Slowly read the text two or three times.

What words, phrases, or ideas capture your attention?

....

....

....

....

2. *Meditatio:* Meditate on the text.

What is God saying to you through these verses? What is he inviting you to? What assurance is he giving you?

....

....

....

....

....

3. *Oratio:* Pray the text.

What do you need to say to God in light of what you hear him saying to you in the passage?

....

....

....

....

....

4. *Contemplatio:* Put the text into practice.

As you think about your day, what is God calling you to?

....

....

....

....

....

LECTIO DIVINA READING FOUR

Date: ....

Location: ....

Passage: ....

1. *Lectio:* Slowly read the text two or three times.
What words, phrases, or ideas capture your attention?

....

....

....

....

2. *Meditatio:* Meditate on the text.
What is God saying to you through these verses? What is he inviting you to? What assurance is he giving you?

....

....

....

....

3. *Oratio:* Pray the text.

What do you need to say to God in light of what you hear him saying to you in the passage?

....

....

....

....

....

4. *Contemplatio:* Put the text into practice.

As you think about your day, what is God calling you to?

....

....

....

....

....

LECTIO DIVINA READING FIVE

Date: ....

Location: ....

Passage: ....

1. *Lectio:* Slowly read the text two or three times.

What words, phrases, or ideas capture your attention?

....

....

....

....

2. *Meditatio:* Meditate on the text.

What is God saying to you through these verses? What is he inviting you to? What assurance is he giving you?

....

....

....

....

3. *Oratio:* Pray the text.

What do you need to say to God in light of what you hear him saying to you in the passage?.

....

....

....

....

....

4. *Contemplatio:* Put the text into practice.

As you think about your day, what is God calling you to?

....

....

....

....

....

TRAVELOGUE FEATURES

OUR JOURNEY

Whether you go halfway around the world or just to the next state, some of your team's most memorable moments will be made on the way to and from the field. As you travel, take a few minutes to record what happened on each leg of your journey. Be sure to record all of those unique travel memories—running to make a connection, immense amounts of luggage and supplies, unexpected delays, the new friend you made while waiting in line, trying to sleep in the train station. These are things that seem really crazy in the moment, but will become memories that make you laugh when you return.

To the Field		
Leg 1	**Leg 2**	**Leg 3**

Date:

From:

To:

Mode of Travel:

Distance:

	To the Field		
	Leg 4	**Leg 5**	**Leg 6**
Date:			
From:			
To:			
Mode of Travel:			
Distance:			

	From the Field		
	Leg 1	**Leg 2**	**Leg 3**
Date:			
From:			
To:			
Mode of Travel:			
Distance:			

	From the Field		
	Leg 4	**Leg 5**	**Leg 6**
Date:			
From:			
To:			
Mode of Travel:			
Distance:			

To and from the Field Travel Memories

To and from the Field Travel Memories

NEW FRIENDS

One of the best parts of any mission trip is the new friends you make. They could be the missionaries you are coming to help, people from other groups and churches who team up to serve with you, national believers you end up working with, or a host family that welcomes you.

Throughout your trip, each time you meet special people you didn't know before, make note of them. Include where or how you met and some contact information if you'd like to be able to connect with them later.

Name	How You Met	Contact Info

Name	How You Met	Contact Info

MISSION MEMORIES

Every trip creates unique memories that you'll want to capture while they are still fresh so that you can share them with others or relive them in future years. Do your best to record things as they happen or grab a few team-mates and work through the list toward the end of your time. Don't worry if you don't have an answer for every question. If something particularly memorable happened, be sure to jot that down too.

1. I shared a room with:

....

....

....

2. The funniest thing that happened on the trip:

....

....

....

3. The best food I ate:

....

....

....

4. The worst/scariest thing I ate:

....

....

....

5. Who gets the award for:

    a. Heaviest Luggage

    ....

    b. Most Unique "Hidden" Skill Set

    ....

    c. Most Memorable "I Can't Believe He/She Did That" Moment

    ....

    d. Hardest Worker

    ....

    e. Best Encourager

    ....

    f. Most Adventurous Eater

    ....

6. Which of the people you served really stood out to you? Why?

    ....

    ....

    ....

7. Your most unusual experience:

    ....

    ....

    ....

8. The biggest surprise about the people you came to serve:

....

....

....

9. The biggest surprise about your team:

....

....

....

10. If your trip had a theme song, what would it be? Why?

....

....

....

11. What is something that you "had to be there" to truly understand?

....

....

....

12. The "quote of the trip" (what was said and by whom):

....

....

....

13. The biggest challenge you faced:

....

....

....

14. The most unexpected thing that made you grateful (eventually):

....

....

....

BY THE NUMBERS

You'd be surprised at just how many things God brings together to make mission trips possible. Do your best to fill out all of the entries, even if you have to make a few educated guesses. Seeing all of the facts and figures that went into your trip is always enlightening.

1. Number of months spent preparing and planning for the trip:

....

2. Amount of support needed for the trip:..

3. Number of people who gave to you and/or prayed for you: ....

4. Number of people on your team from your church: ....

5. Total number of people on the trip:...

6. Number of days the trip took: ....

7. Total number of miles traveled: ....

8. Number of people served on the trip: ....

9. Number of hours spent serving others on the trip (i.e. spent in "ministry time"):

....

10. Number of types of transportation you used: ....

11. Number of fast food meals eaten: ....

12. Number of cities/states/countries you traveled over or through:

....

13. Number of people you thought would never finish the trip:

....

AFTER THE TRIP

THE TRIP IS DONE!

Congratulations! You've survived! You're home—or nearly there!

Over the last several months you've raised support, planned, prepared, and hopefully had a great experience loving and serving others while you were away.

But in many ways, the real work of your mission trip is just now beginning. Finding ways to take what you learned and experienced on the trip and connecting it to your everyday life is crucial for all short-term mission experiences. Unless you are intentional about this, the spiritual lessons and passions awakened by the trip will fade with your memories of your experiences. Despite the time, effort, and expense involved, it's likely that your trip will feel like little more than a week of work unless you set aside time to reflect, process, and talk with God about it.

In light of that, I encourage you to think of the three debrief exercises that follow as *one of the most important parts of your mission experience*. They will help you process what you've experienced and capture the key things God has shown you. They will also invite you to prayerfully consider how Jesus wants to draw you deeper into his mission of redeeming and restoring a lost and broken world. And they will give you suggestions on how to live on mission now that you are back.

Take a few minutes right now to look through your calendar and pencil in dates to complete each debrief. Plan on spending roughly forty-five minutes on each session.

DEBRIEF ONE | MAKING SENSE OF WHAT YOU'VE SEEN

Debrief One focuses on your experiences on the trip and the key things you learned while both are still fresh in your mind.

Debrief One should be completed on your way home or within the first week of your return.

I'll complete Debrief One on: ....

DEBRIEF TWO | THE GOSPEL IN AND THROUGH YOU TO OTHERS

Debrief Two focuses on the lessons you learned, the passions you developed, and how they connect with your everyday life to help you continue living on mission.

Debrief Two should be completed four to six weeks after your return.

I'll complete Debrief Two on: ....

DEBRIEF THREE | THE ONGOING JOURNEY

Debrief Three will help you review your plan and suggest other, long-term ways to keep staying engaged with missions and local outreach.

Debrief Three should be completed six months after you have returned.

I'll complete Debrief Three on: ....

God was at work in your life long before you ever left, and he'll continue to be at work in the days and months ahead, but your mission trip represents a unique opportunity for spiritual growth and engagement. I hope you'll give yourself the gift of spending some time talking with God about what he's done in you and asking him how he'd like to continue to work through you.

DEBRIEF ONE | MAKING SENSE OF WHAT YOU'VE SEEN

Timeframe for Completion: On the way home or during your first week back

INTRODUCTION

Remember the spectrum of emotions you felt as you prepared for your trip a few weeks ago? As you reenter your home culture and the routines of "normal life," you may be experiencing a similar whirlwind of feelings.

Use the following journaling assignment to reflect on your trip and identify the insights you've gained about yourself, about God, and about mission. Taking this intentional time of reflection will be a crucial first step in connecting your short-term trip to your life back home. It will serve you well as you tell others what happened during your week of ministry.

PART 1. EXPECTATIONS AND REALITY

Read your responses from *Part 1: Inventory of Needs and Hopes* (pp. 7–9) in the Pre-Trip Assignments, then answer the following questions. Be as specific as you can, citing particular incidents, locations, and people. Use this book's devotional and journaling sections to jog your memory if needed.

1. What were your biggest fears or struggles going into the trip?

....

....

....

....

- What actually happened on the trip in these areas?

....

....

....

2. What were your biggest hopes or desires for how God would work on the trip?

....

....

....

....

- What actually happened on the trip in these areas?

....

....

....

PART 2. WHAT DID YOU LEARN ABOUT YOURSELF?

As you reflect on what you learned about yourself during the trip, answer the following questions:

1. Where did you feel like you had "poured Miracle-Gro®" on your sin during the trip? (See if you can list a specific incident or sin pattern.) What did this reveal to you about the ongoing level of unbelief that is present in your heart?

....

....

....

....

2. What was the most significant time when you had to "step out in faith" to do something on the trip?

....

....

....

....

- What were you feeling before you did it?

....

....

....

- How did God meet you?

....

....

....

- What happened as a result?

....

....

....

3. Think of a few times when you saw God specifically use you on the trip. It could have been by helping or encouraging a teammate, loving one of the people you came to serve, or giving you the solution to a difficult problem or situation.

- What happened?

....

....

....

- What was it like to experience God using you in this way?

....

....

....

PART 3. WHAT DID YOU LEARN ABOUT GOD?

Getting to see God work in us and through us in unexpected and exciting ways is one of the great experiences of a mission trip. Take ten or fifteen minutes now to sit and listen to God, considering the following question. Be patient and listen for his voice, recording whatever things the Holy Spirit brings to mind.

> "God, in light of all that you did and showed me on the trip, what do you want to say to me right now that I should remember as I reengage my normal life?"

GETTING READY TO TELL YOUR STORY

In the coming days and weeks, many will want to hear about your mission experience. Different people will want to hear about your trip in varying degrees of depth. Using your reflections above, spend a few minutes writing a one-minute version, a five-minute version, and a twenty-minute version of your experience.

I'd also recommend asking a trusted friend to meet with you for an hour so that you can run through your different summaries and process things out loud. You may find that you've forgotten to include important elements, or that some parts of your experience are best kept private. Having talked through your trip with a close friend can also help if you are nervous about telling others about your trip.

Key details for a twenty-minute story

....

....

....

Key details for a five-minute story

....

....

....

Key details for a one-minute story

....

....

....

DON'T FORGET to write a note to your support team, thanking them for their generosity and their prayers. Be sure to include a few of the insights that you wrote down in the previous sections.

DEBRIEF TWO | THE GOSPEL IN AND THROUGH YOU TO OTHERS

Timeframe for Completion: Four to six weeks after returning

INTRODUCTION

By now the dust has settled, the suitcases are (hopefully!) unpacked, jet lag is over, and life likely feels "back to normal." As you process the difference between "everyday life" and "that trip I took a month ago," use the following journaling exercises to consider these questions: Now that I'm home, how do I engage differently with my own heart and my need for the gospel? And with the world's needs?

> *Note to Leaders:* Now would be a great time for a group reunion and debrief. You could incorporate the plans people will be developing in Part 2 (below) into the group conversation, and help those with similar passions to connect with each other.

PART 1. THE GOSPEL IN ME (JOURNALING EXERCISE)

One of the gifts of short-term mission is the opportunity to see our sin and neediness more clearly. As we said earlier, going to the mission field is like "pouring Miracle-Gro® on your sin." Your time in cross-cultural ministry probably revealed some deep heart-level needs that you may have never noticed before—needs that were always there but hard to see in your everyday life.

1. As I consider the spiritual needs I felt during my trip, where do I see similar strands of unbelief now, in my life back home? What new corners of neediness do I see in my heart?

....

....

....

....

2. How is Jesus meeting me in the midst of these struggles? What specific things can I receive from the gospel as I face unbelief in my life right now?

....

....

....

....

PART 2. THE GOSPEL THROUGH ME (JOURNALING + PLANNING EXERCISE)

It always seems easier to reach out to those who don't know Jesus when we are on a mission trip. After all, that's why "we" came—to serve "them." But the truth is that when we are following Jesus's lead on how to love people, there is no "us" and "them." There is only "us"—people who desperately need Jesus, every day, to be their Savior, to lead and guide, to heal and empower. Some of us know this, some of us don't. But we are all sinners in need of a Savior. After all, being a Christian doesn't remove your need for Jesus; it simply shows you how amazingly he meets that need.

One lasting impact of every mission trip should be a greater desire and ability to live "on mission" as part of our everyday lives. Take some time to think through the following questions. As you do, really pray and really listen to what God is saying. It may be helpful to recall a time on your trip when you felt totally helpless but then saw God answer your prayers and meet your needs in clear and overwhelming ways.

1. What needs do I see in the world around me? In my church? In my neighborhood? In my social circles? In my workplace? In the world?

    ....

    ....

    ....

    ....

2. Where might God be calling me into mission back home in deeper ways?
    For each category below, try to list one or two concrete actions that you sense God is calling you to do. Then share your list with a few friends and ask them to pray for you.

    If you need suggestions for what action steps look like in each heading, see the "Practical Helps" list at the end of Debrief Two.

    God, how are you drawing me to **pray** differently?

    ....

    ....

    ....

    God, where are you calling me to **serve** more intentionally?

    ....

    ....

    ....

God, where are you encouraging me to **give** more generously?

....

....

....

God, where are you asking me to **go** boldly?

....

....

....

PART 3. JESUS WITH ME (JOURNALING EXERCISE)

1. What feels challenging and risky about the plan I created? How is this pushing me to be more dependent on Jesus? Just as I got ready for my short-term trip and felt needy, how do I feel needy now, as I get ready to step deeper into mission in my local context?

....

....

....

....

2. How does the gospel speak to my specific fears and needs? Pray for Jesus to meet you here; pray for his partnership as you come alongside him in loving the lost.

....

....

....

....

PRACTICAL HELPS

We've brainstormed a "starter list" of ways you may want to consider praying, serving, giving, and going. Feel free to use this as a jumping-off point as you create your plan in Part 2 above, but don't feel limited to choosing things from the lists. God can use you any way he wants!

Praying

- *Ask to be added to the prayer update lists for missionaries or ministries you encountered on the trip.* Now that you've had a chance to meet them and see what they do, you can pray in deeper ways for them.
- *Sign up for prayer updates from all of the missionaries your church supports.* Even if you haven't met them yet, it's likely that they will visit your church sometime when they're home.
- *If your church doesn't have a system for distributing and updating missionary prayer requests, consider volunteering to start and maintain one.* With a little cutting and pasting, you can help those in your church to see all of the prayer needs in one place.
- *Lead your small group or Sunday school class in "adopting" a missionary/ministry for a year; make a point of praying for them when you are together.* They may even be able to join you for a short phone or video call during one of your meetings.
- *Choose a region of the world that you feel drawn to and become a "prayer expert" on the needs of God's people in that region.* It could be connected to your trip or someplace God has put on your heart. Seeing how God is involved with people from many countries in a particular region of the world is a great way to get a broader perspective on his purposes. Examples could include house churches in China; ministry to North African Muslims; the needs of immigrant communities in Western countries; sex trafficking in Asia, etc.
- *Make it a point to write a personal email to one of the missionaries you met or one that you or your church supports.* Let them know how much you appreciate what they are doing and ask if there are particular ways you can pray for their spiritual growth. You'd be surprised at how often the spiritual needs of

missionaries are overlooked when people ask for a report on their work.

- *Consider using the resources from websites* like Operation World (www.operationworld.org) or The Voice of the Martyrs (www.persecution.com) to gain information about specific countries and prayer needs.
- *No matter what you do, use your own mission trip experience to pray more deeply and personally for people.* Once you've met people serving on the field, it's a lot easier to see missions as a large family of relationships instead of separate ministries and causes.
- *Consider being the "prayer champion" for future short-term teams that your church sends.* Offer to coordinate prayer requests, update your leaders, and recruit others to pray during the trip.

Serving

- *Adopt a missionary or missionary team for a year.* You can do this by yourself, as a family, with friends, or with your small group or Sunday school class. Find out how you can pray for them, but also how you can minister to them and encourage them.
- *Send a care package.* All missionaries have things they like that are almost impossible to get where they live. Food or spices, DVDs, puzzles and games, clothes, high quality tools and repair items—there is always a list of things that will lift a missionary's spirit. Mostly they'll just be grateful that someone back home is thinking of them.
- *Consider serving on your church's missions committee.* Now that you've had a chance to see things firsthand, perhaps you can be of service to the rest of your church by helping them support, stay connected to, and pray for missionaries.
- *Go out of your way to meet the needs of missionaries while at home.* When missionaries are on home assignment or travel-ing to meet supporters, they often need a whole range of things, from temporary accommodation and transportation, to help with figuring out schooling options and setting up new cell

phones. Tip: contact your missionary and ask specifically what she needs; don't offer a generic "Let me know if I can help."

- *Offer your expertise to missionaries while they are home or on the field.* Are you a whiz with taxes? Run your own IT consulting agency? Know how to research the best digital camera to use in rugged, humid conditions? Inevitably you are good at something that a missionary could use help with. The better you know your missionaries, the more you'll learn how you can help.

- *Donate your air miles to help missionaries get home for special occasions.* One of the hardest things for missionaries is missing important family/life events due to the expense of air travel. Offering extra frequent flier miles, often good for flights, car rental, and lodging, is a tangible way to help.

- *Let a missionary family use your vacation or rental property for free, or donate a week or two at a timeshare you own.* Finding places to just "be away," even when they are home, is huge need and challenge on a limited budget. Offering missionaries a place to go and rest is a tremendous blessing.

- *Offer to collect and ship needed ministry items to a missionary.* Fifty soccer balls? School supplies? New socks and underwear? You'd be surprised what you'll hear about when you start asking. Even when a missionary has funds for the items, getting them into their country is difficult. Having someone who is willing to help is a huge blessing. Be sure to ask your missionary about any taxes or import duties they may have to pay for goods shipped to them and include that cost in your budget.

Giving

- *Evaluate your monthly giving to missionaries.* Every missionary is in need of monthly supporters. After you have met your giving commitments to your local church, pray about supporting a new missionary or increasing your giving to missionaries you currently support.

- *Evaluate your giving to special projects.* Setting aside money throughout the year or using some of the money from bonuses, tax refunds, or rebates is a great way to bless missionaries with one-time gifts. There are always unexpected expenses on the field and *you* can be part of God's answer to their prayers.

- *Sponsor a project or give to a missionary as a family.* Getting children involved in learning about missionaries, other countries, and God's kingdom is a great way to introduce them to missions. Children can earn money from chores or through fundraisers to help contribute to your giving.

- *Help your church organize a special giving project for children.* Help your children's Sunday school or VBS program find a way to collect money and give to missions. It could be a project or a missionary, but getting kids involved in giving is a great way to not only help missionaries, but to foster a child's interest in missions.

- *Help your church organize a special project to support.* Find out if one of your missionaries has a special funding need for a particular project. Then offer to organize the youth group to run a fundraising event (a golf outing, bake sale, etc.) to meet that need. This raises needed money and also highlights your ministry partners and their work.

- *Fast for a month!* Relax, you can still eat. Consider giving up one of your little luxuries for a month—your daily latte, that trip through the drive-thru window—and donating the money you save to a missions cause. Every time you'd normally spend that money, it's a good reminder to pray for the people you want to support.

- *Offer to host a support party for a visiting missionary.* Missionaries are regularly in need of opportunities to make new contacts, explain their work, and invite people to join them in prayer and financial support. Be bold and offer to host a party for them. Invite your friends so they'll have a ready and waiting audience.

Going
- *Do everything you can to make sure your pastors can visit mission fields.* Whether it's encouraging them to go, offering to mow their lawn while they're gone, or offering to watch their children so their spouse can join them, regularly having your

pastors visit the mission fields you support is an essential part of keeping the vision and passion for missions in front of your congregation.

- *Help your church take its next mission trip.* Offer to help recruit, make a video, invite people to the information sessions, keep the books for the team. You may not be ready or able to go again, but you can help others get there.

- *Encourage people to go.* Everyone has a million reasons why they haven't taken a mission trip. Help them overcome those reasons by winsomely sharing your own experience.

- *Find internationals living near you and reach out to them.* Often people from countries that are closed—or nearly so—to missionaries are open to talk about spiritual things when they are living away from home. Offer to host a foreign family, invite them over for lunch, help them figure out how to register for the local youth soccer team, or volunteer to teach English.

- *If you have in-demand skills (medical, dental, construction etc.), consider taking regular trips every year or every other year.* By working with the same group repeatedly, you can minimize time and effort and maximize effects. You can also be a bridge for others with similar skills who don't know how to get involved.

- *Consider going for one to six months.* A week or two is great, but often the needs of the field are better met when you can offer needed services or help for a longer period of time. Many mission agencies can connect you with a team or service area that you have a passion for.

- *Consider going . . . forever!* Not everyone is called to be a missionary. But some are! Maybe as a result of your trip (or a longer stay), you need to set aside time to listen and see if God is calling you to longer service. It's not an "all or nothing" proposition. Take one step at a time and recruit a prayer team to walk with you.

- *If you are thinking about exploring a future in missions, Serge offers missions opportunities all the way from two months to long term.* Find more info at Serge.org.

DEBRIEF THREE | THE ONGOING JOURNEY

Timeframe for Completion: Six months after you return

INTRODUCTION

Can you believe that it's been six months since your mission trip? Often the hustle and bustle of daily life can dim our memories of the spiritual lessons and experiences that were crystal clear to us when we first returned.

In the first debrief, we asked you to record some of those experiences and emotions. In the second debrief we asked you to reflect more deliberately on what God had done and, just as importantly, what he still wanted to do through you to expand his kingdom. This debrief is intended to give you a chance to sit with God and honestly ask, "How is it going? Am I doing the things that I sensed you wanted me to do?"

Don't forget the lessons you learned through the daily devotionals—you're no more of a spiritual superstar now than you were on the trip. It's likely that you've had plans you haven't carried out, or you've made mistakes along the way. That's okay. Jesus knows. He's with you. He cares. And he's just as able to use you here and now as he was six months ago on the trip.

1. Review the plan you came up with on pp. 124–25 for praying, serving, giving, and going. Then spend a few minutes answering the following questions:
    Praying differently . . .

    How have you been doing with your plans for praying differently?

    ....

    ....

    ....

    Are there items you listed that you still haven't gotten to? If so, can you make some tangible plans right now to get to them?

    ....

....

....

Serving more intentionally. . .

How have you been doing with your plans for serving more intentionally?

....

....

....

Are there items you listed that you still haven't gotten to? If so, can you make some tangible plans right now to get to them?

....

....

....

Giving more generously . . .

How have you been doing with your plans for giving more generously?

....

....

....

Are there items you listed that you still haven't gotten to? If so, can you make some tangible plans right now to get to them?

....

....

....

Going boldly . . .

How have you been doing with your plans for going boldly?

....

....

....

Are there items you listed that you still haven't gotten to? If so, can you make some tangible plans right now to get to them?

....

....

....

2. As you have tried to work through your plan, where have you seen it reveal more of your need for Christ? How has God been meeting you in these areas?

....

....

....

....

WHAT DO YOU WANT ME TO DO FOR YOU?

We started this book by looking at Jesus's encounter with the blind man Bartimaeus. Jesus heard Bartimaeus's cries acknowledging him as the Messiah; he saw his blindness; he knew his heart. He then asked Bartimaeus a revealing question: "What do you want me to do for you?" (Mark 10:51). Jesus wasn't asking because he didn't know what Bartimaeus needed. As he made his way to Jerusalem to die for the sins of his people, Jesus was exceedingly clear about what Bartimaeus needed. What Jesus was really asking was, "Bartimaeus, do *you* really know what your deepest needs are?"

Through your trip and your time with God getting ready, working through the devotionals and debriefing, I hope that you too have started to see your deepest needs. I have to admit that when Jesus asks, "What do you want me to do for you, Patric?" I'm still prone to ask for things that will make me "better" so that I don't need to rely on Jesus all the time! So often, my heart wants God to bless my efforts, agendas, and methods so that I don't have to rely on his love, goodness, and provision. An independent heart like mine doesn't want to receive something I don't deserve, even when that something is love. I want to earn it, and receiving grace as a gift is humbling to my proud and fearful heart that would rather trust itself.

Bartimaeus, however, had no illusions about his ability to earn his way with God or with other men. He asks for, and receives, his eyesight because he knows that his deepest need is reconciliation with God, which can only happen by fully relying on him.

After he healed Bartimaeus, Jesus explicitly released him from any further obligations, letting him know that he could go on his way. But Bartimaeus's way has now become Jesus's way; he joins Jesus and his disciples as they move down the road.

Whenever grace moves into our lives, it always moves us beyond ourselves. In the years ahead, I hope that you'll revisit these pages from time to time. I hope you'll remember the good and the bad of your journey. But mostly I hope you'll remember those special days when you stood on the front lines of the kingdom and saw God and yourself more clearly, so that you too will travel the road with Jesus, loving what he loves, and wanting what he wants.

mission
propelled by good news

At Serge we believe that mission begins through the gospel of Jesus Christ bringing God's grace into the lives of believers. This good news also sustains and empowers us to cross nations and cultures to bring the gospel of grace to those whom God is calling to Himself.

As a cross-denominational, reformed, sending agency with more than 200 missionaries and 25 teams in 5 continents, we are always looking for people who are ready to take the next step in sharing Christ, through:

- **Short-term Teams**: One to two-week trips oriented around serving overseas ministries while equipping the local church for mission
- **Internships:** Eight-week to nine-month opportunities to learn about missions through serving with our overseas ministry teams
- **Apprenticeships:** Intensive 12–24 month training and ministry opportunities for those discerning their call to cross-cultural ministry
- **Career:** One- to five-year appointments designed to nurture you for a lifetime of ministry

 Grace at the Fray

Visit us online at: serge.org/mission

www.newgrowthpress.com

spiritual renewal
resources for you

Disciples who are motivated and empowered by grace to reach out to a broken world are handmade, not mass-produced. Serge intentionally grows disciples through curriculum, discipleship experiences, and training programs.

Resources for Every Stage of Growth

Serge offers grace-based, gospel-centered studies for every stage of the Christian journey. Every level of our materials focuses on essential aspects of how the Spirit transforms and motivates us through the gospel of Jesus Christ.

- **101**: The Gospel-Centered Series
  Gospel-centered studies on Christian growth, community, work, parenting, and more.
- **201**: The Gospel Transformation Series
  These studies go a step deeper into Gospel transformation, involve homework and more in-depth Bible study
- **301**: The Sonship Course and Serge Individual Mentoring

Mentored Sonship

For more than 25 years Serge has been discipling ministry leaders around the world through our Sonship course to help them experience the freedom and joy of having the gospel transform every part of their lives. A personal discipler will help you apply what you are learning to the daily struggles and situations you face, as well as, model what a gospel-centered faith looks and feels like.

Discipler Training Course

Serge's Discipler Training Course helps you gain biblical understanding and practical wisdom you need to disciple others so they experience substantive, lasting growth in their lives. Available for onsite training or via distance learning, our training programs are ideal for ministry leaders, small group leaders or those seeking to grow in their ability to disciple effectively.

 Grace at the Fray

Find more resources at serge.org